Baseball Fans Stand and Cheer for
The Tall Mexican: The Life of Hank Aguirre

"As a personal friend of Aguirre, Copley is privy to **fascinating details** about him that raise this biography **above standard fare.** Descriptions of the subject's childhood are **rich in detail,** and the baseball highlights not only give **a vivid sense of the game** during the 1960s but also include personal anecdotes from legends such as Leo Durocher and Mickey Lolich. Meticulous, humble, and ethical, **Aguirre proves a most worthy biographical subject and inspiring hero.**"
    —*Booklist*

"*The Tall Mexican* chronicles the full life of this baseball player turned business owner . . . The book is a **fair,** warts-and-all biography of a man who didn't have many. **Very well written,** *The Tall Mexican* is a fast read."
    —Rick Mendosa, *Hispanic Business* magazine

"America is a country of immigrants, with a culture built from every corner of the globe . . . For **pure inspiration,** there's *The Tall Mexican*, Robert E. Copley's **moving** biography of ballplayer, businessman, and humanitarian Hank Aguirre . . . [who was] born in Azusa to Mexican immigrant parents."
    — Kevin Baxter, *The Los Angeles Times*

(please turn the page for more rave reviews)

"I read *The Tall Mexican* in two gulps . . . I don't know who Bob Copley is, but he's **a real writer.** The Hank Aguirre he portrays is a charming, clever, industrious, generous, high-spirited, two-enterprise success. He is also hot-tempered, and sometimes abusive . . . an interesting mix of rugged individualism and affirmative action . . . a **fascinating** bundle of contradictions."
> —Zev Chafets, author of
> *Devil's Night and Other True Tales of Detroit*

"This book is an **important** Hispanic biography."
> —*Book Report*

"Not only an **engaging and inspirational** story . . . but also a reminder about the rich diversity of Hispanic America and especially of those Americans of Mexican heritage who have achieved so much in this society."
> —Prof. Lester Langley, author of
> *MexAmerica: Two Countries, One Future*

"This **extremely readable** account of the great 1960s Mexican-American athlete, while geared to young adults, is for all age groups. . . . Aguirre's life story shows that heroes can make a difference, both as role models and by giving back to the community. [A] **fine** book."
> —Mary Helen Ponce, *Saludos Hispanos* magazine

The Tall Mexican

The Life of Hank Aguirre
All-Star Pitcher, Businessman, Humanitarian

Robert E. Copley

With a Foreword by José F. Niño

PIÑATA BOOKS
ARTE PÚBLICO PRESS
HOUSTON, TEXAS
2000

This volume is made possible through grants from the Rockefeller Foundation, the National Endowment for the Arts (a federal agency), the Andrew W. Mellon Foundation, and the Cultural Arts Council of Houston–Harris County.

Piñata Books
An Imprint of Arte Público Press
University of Houston
452 Cullen Performance Hall
Houston, Texas 77204-2004

Cover design by Ken Bullock
Cover art by William C. Klemm

Photographs from Aguirre family archives.
Reproduced by kind permission of Pamela Aguirre.

"You Are Your Own Best Union," by Raoul Lowery Contreras,
originally appeared in the June 15, 1995 *El Central* (Detroit).
Reprinted by express permission of the author.

∞ The paper used in this publication meets the requirements of the American National Standard for Information Sciences—Permanence of Paper for Printed Library Materials, ANSI Z39.48-1984.

5 6 7 8 9 0 1 2 3 4   12 11 10 9 8 7 6 5 4 3

There is a destiny which makes us brothers,
None goes his way alone.
What we send out into the lives of others
Comes back into our own.

–Edwin Markham
(from "A Creed")

To Hank's children

Jill, Pam, Rance, and Robin

who hold Hank's legacy in their hearts.

Contents

Illustrations

Foreword

HERO, MENTOR, ROLE MODEL. From an early age, Hank Aguirre was destined to have all three titles. I know this to be true from the stories I have heard of his youth, during which he laid a strong foundation for the rest of his life. At 4 AM, he would make deliveries to the many clients of the "Aguirre Tortillas Factory" in California. These deliveries were made on foot—mostly running—every day of the week, before Hank went to school. The discipline he gained in these workouts prepared him for his journey to the major leagues, where he thrilled many baseball fans with his talent, and sparked dreams of opportunity in the eyes of the children and youths who watched him. Later, as a coach, he shared his knowledge and expertise with many aspiring younger athletes.

I met Hank in the early 1980s. By then he had moved on to succeed in yet another challenging area: He was a successful small business owner. He founded Mexican Industries in Detroit, and did work for the auto industry. In its early stages, Mexican Industries produced small, stamped, metal parts. Later, he decided to shift his company to a cut-and-sew operation, and it has remained in that business ever since. Hank hired most of his employees from the Mexican-American community in Detroit. As his business grew, he reinvested in his community, helping to bring economic development and opportunity to the place where his employees lived.

Hank had a caring nature, and it showed in the relationship he developed with his employees at Mexican Industries. Each morning he would walk through the plant, greeting each person by name, inquiring about his or her health and family. It was a genuine concern, and his employees knew it. Together, they built a great company.

In 1987, Hank was named Businessman of the Year by the United States Hispanic Chamber of Commerce (USHCC). He was also recognized many times by other organizations and institutions. He assisted many people with their own business-es as he shared his knowledge in seminars. Hank showed a great deal of devotion to his church, his family, his communi-ty, and his business. I was grateful for all his support as a member of, and business advisor to, the USHCC.

To the immediate family of Hank Aguirre: Please know that we share in your sorrow, and that we miss him, too! As we look on and celebrate Hank's life, we reflect on his teachings, for we have learned from him. To Hank Aguirre, our hero, mentor, and role model: *¡Gracias por todo amigo!*

> *José F. Niño*
> *President and Chief Executive Officer*
> *U. S. Hispanic Chamber of Commerce*

Preface and Acknowledgments

I first met Hank Aguirre in the fall of 1962. Hank had just finished a sensational year with the Detroit Tigers as a starting pitcher. He made the American League's All-Star team that year with an ERA of 2.21. I was a writer for a marketing agency that had offices in Detroit and had hired Hank, during his off-season, to help its account executives open doors to the automotive industry. I helped Hank to write up proposals for new business.

Our friendship spanned more than thirty years. He, above all my friends, had the most profound influence on my life. I was his publicist during his eleven-year stint with the Detroit Tigers, and when he formed Mexican Industries in 1979, he asked me to help him with his communications effort. We remained close until his untimely death in his suburban Detroit home on Labor Day, September 5, 1994.

It's impossible to write anything about Hank without writing about love at the same time, because the two were inseparable. I am not alone in that love, for he gave each of us who knew him the same remarkable gifts: his vision, his integrity, his wisdom, his forgiveness, his generosity, his great humor, and—above all—his love.

For several years before his death, I tried to convince Hank to allow me to help him put his autobiography together, for here was a man who had two separate and distinctly successful careers. I believed (like many others who knew him) that Hank's story would be an inspiration to all those—especially his fellow Hispanics—who were finding life tough and were struggling to climb up from the bottom of the economic ladder.

Characteristically, Hank thought a book about himself would be self-serving. He couldn't see how his life was extraordinary. "You won't find my face on Mount Rushmore," was one of his typical self-deprecating responses to the applause that would follow a speech he had delivered, or to an award he had received. Finally, several months into his final illness, he agreed to go ahead with his autobiography "as soon as I feel better." That time never came. Within a year he was laid to rest in an old mission cemetery in San Gabriel, California—the town in which he had grown up. Inscribed on his headstone are the words *¡Tu Espiritu Vive!* (Your Spirit Lives!). And it does.

Improving the lives of his fellow Hispanic Americans was a passion with Hank Aguirre. He mortgaged his home, placed most of his personal assets on the line, and dedicated his organizational and entrepreneurial skills to that end. His success is evident in the uplifted quality of life within the Hispanic community where he located his business. Hank was proud of his Hispanic heritage, and he was always true to his fellow Hispanics. In the process of building Mexican Industries, he ultimately became a wealthy man, but he never forgot his roots.

With Hank's death, his projected autobiography instead became a biography. Since I wanted it to be an *authorized* biography, I sought permission from his children to proceed. They granted me that permission. I went down many blind alleys in pursuit of Hank's story, but on the whole my research and interviews brought me knowledge, rich in detail, far beyond even my own long personal experience of Hank.

I acknowledge and extend my thanks and appreciation to the many who gave of their time so generously during my research. I extend special thanks to Hank's brothers Joseph and Richard; to his sisters Irene and Helen, and their husbands, Manuel and David; to Hank's daughters, Pamela, Jill, and Robin; and to his son, Rance. I also thank my wife, Ruth, for her diligence with the laborious chore of incorporating proofreading corrections into the manuscript.

Others to whom I owe my thanks and appreciation include Tina Aguirre, Ben Cordoba, Bill Freehan, Bill Reedy, Bill Flynn, Charlie and Gwen Briley, Clint Lauer, Diane Finkel, Don Lund, Dr. Bruce Redman, Barbara Aguirre, Ernie Harwell, Father Don Worthy, Ferguson Jenkins, Fred Smith, Gilbert and Sara Aguirre, Glenn Beckert, Gracie Zuniga, Jay Bocci, Jeanne Parzuchowski, Jerry Coyne, Jim Merkhofer, Jim Hickman, Jim Northrup, John Livingstone, John Noonan, Kevin Collins, Linda Valli, Martha Silva, Jim Reedy, Mayor Coleman Young, Mickey Lolich, Reno Bertoia, Irene Estrada, Richard Burtle, Stan and Mary Clarke, Ted Williams, Willie Horton, Miriam Herrando, Tom Kerr, Terry Henderson, Pat Guerrero, Esther Jiminez, Dalia Garcia, Vicki Sieracki, Harold R. Roehrig, and Joe Schmidt.

Because of the breadth of my research, I have undoubtedly overlooked some people who contributed in one way or another to this biography. To those I have missed, I apologize; I am grateful to them for their generous contributions. I also thank those who supported me in those dark and lonely moments that come to most writers when they hit mental blocks or begin to doubt if their efforts are worthwhile. All their contributions helped immeasurably to allow me to build this account of the unique life of Hank Aguirre.

Bob Copley
Royal Oak, Michigan

Chapter One
The View from the Mound

On the evening of July 21, 1993, at the Westin Hotel in Detroit, Michigan, Hank Aguirre was honored by the National Council of La Raza at its Silver Anniversary convention. In recognition of his life's work, Hank—a former Detroit Tiger All-Star pitcher, a successful businessman, and a humanitarian whom I was honored to call my good friend for many years—received the Roberto Clemente Award for Excellence.

Clemente, a native of Puerto Rico, had been a star outfielder for the Pittsburgh Pirates from 1955 to 1972. Not only had he excelled in his profession, he had cared about others as well. One of his dreams—fulfilled after many years—was to found a Sports City, or Cuidad Deportiva, where Puerto Rican youths could participate in all kinds of sports and other activities. Following a terrible earthquake in Nicaragua, Clemente chartered an airplane to carry medical supplies and food to the people there. Shortly after its takeoff, on the last day of 1972, the plane had crashed at sea, and no bodies were ever recovered. Clemente, who had been only 38 years old, was elected to the Baseball Hall of Fame in remembrance of both his excellence as a player (3,000 hits!) and his civic-minded efforts.

Today, the Roberto Clemente Award for Excellence is presented each year to a sports figure who is committed to the advancement of Hispanic Americans. There couldn't have been a better choice than Hank Aguirre. At six feet, four inches, "The Tall Mexican," as sportwriters called him, had been a

1

magnificent athlete, and his driving passion was to help fellow Hispanic Americans succeed.

Applause rolled over the great ballroom as he was introduced, and the audience of about 1,600 rose in a standing ovation. Even so, Hank towered above the crowd of well-wishers as he worked his way to the stage, pausing only to accept individual congratulations and shake outstretched hands.

He mounted the riser and strode directly to the podium. When he turned to face his audience, the applause surged. Beaming, he raised his arms to acknowledge the tribute. Standing up there, Hank may have thought back to his years on the pitcher's mound. He may have remembered his long struggles afterwards in starting up his company, Mexican Industries. And perhaps he remembered times when the crowds had not been so friendly.

Hank understood and appreciated the power of words. I had worked with him for many years—first when he was a ballplayer, and later during his business career—helping to draft his letters, memos, and speeches. In our discussions, Hank was always particular about finding the right word, the one that would capture precisely what he wanted to convey.

For his speech at this gathering, Hank had told me, he wanted to stress the contributions that Hispanic Americans make to the economic health of their home, the United States. He wanted to emphasize that Hispanics wanted no special breaks. Working together, Hank and I went through several drafts. At last he was satisfied with this crucial message, this essential declaration: *We are not looking for handouts. We are looking for equal opportunity.*

The applause continued for several minutes before finally subsiding. At last, the audience waited in absolute silence. Then Hank Aguirre—once a gangly Mexican-American kid who had labored for his dad making tortillas in the back of the family store in Azusa, California—told the crowd:

> In my lifetime, I have seen us grow from a bunch of isolated people, struggling for whatever was available to keep our families together—food on the table, a place to call home—to a major force in the political and economic environment of this great country.
>
> At the turn of the twenty-first century, we will be the largest minority in the United States . . .
>
> We are becoming better educated, and more highly skilled. And as we see the progress we are making, our determination and confidence in what we can do grows.
>
> Listen, corporate America! We are not looking for handouts! We are not looking for easy ways to achieve our goals. We know achievement can come only through diligence and intelligent effort. We ask for nothing more than an equal opportunity to compete.
>
> We no longer look to the future with hopelessness and despair! We look to the future with hope and confidence. The challenges are still out there for us to meet, that's for sure. But I ask you to remember that each of us is like an angel with just one wing: We can fly only by embracing one another.

Chapter Two
Learning How to Slide

Hank Aguirre's family traces its roots back to the Basque region of northern Spain. The family story is that Francisco Aguirre, a cavalry officer in *conquistador* Hernando Cortez's expeditionary force, came ashore near what is now Vera Cruz, on Mexico's eastern coast, in the year 1519 A.D. Searching for gold, Cortez cut a wide and brutal swath on his way northwest to what today is Mexico City. There he claimed the entire land for Spain. The native Indians, having never seen horses before, believed that each mounted rider and his horse were a single, godlike being. Cortez's invading Spaniards overthrew the Aztec empire in the relatively short time of two years.

At the start of the twentieth century, Hank's grandfather, Leno San Roman Aguirre, homesteaded a few acres of land at Encarnacion de Diaz in the state of Jalisco, Mexico. Hank's father, Joseph, was born there in 1902. Shortly thereafter, the family moved to the town of Zacatecas, in central Mexico.

From Zacatecas, the family migrated a few years later to the United States. It is uncertain exactly why Hank's grandfather subjected his family to the arduous and dangerous trek. However, it may have been for their own safety. In November of 1910, the Mexican Revolution erupted. Under the reformer Francisco Madero, an armed uprising overthrew the repressive government of President Porfirio Diaz. The revolution offered the prospect of hope to Mexico's common people—but it also led to years of civil upheaval, horrendous living conditions, and bloodshed.

According to one family story, Leno San Roman Aguirre's decision was triggered when the bandit and revolutionary Francisco (Pancho) Villa, with a half-hundred of his mounted troops, thundered into Zacatecas late one sizzling afternoon and drew up in front of a saddle shop. (Villa was considered a hero by some; a bank-robbing, horse-stealing villain by others.) Without dismounting, Villa told the shop owner that he needed saddles for his men. The saddler was Leno San Roman Aguirre.

According to family folklore, Aguirre told Pancho Villa that not only would he make the needed saddles, he would make them at a very good price. Villa then reminded him that everything for the revolution was *donated*—in the name of liberty and justice. The people, he added, would be grateful for the saddlemaker's generosity. Then Villa drew a pistol from his holster, placed the muzzle against Leno San Roman Aguirre's chest, and asked, *"¿Adonde esta su corazon?"* (Where is your heart?)

Shortly thereafter, the Aguirre family quietly left Zacatecas, boarding a train for the long trip north through the Sonora Desert to the border town of El Paso, Texas.

From El Paso, the family moved several times—first to Phoenix, Arizona, and then to California: Escondido, then Watts, and finally Azusa, where they settled. Around Azusa were vast groves of orange trees, and the family found work picking the land's golden bounty. As crop followers, or *braceros,* the Aguirres had arrived.

Under these difficult conditions, Hank's father, Joseph, achieved the equivalent of a sixth-grade education. Joseph discerned the dead-end, seasonal, and migratory nature of harvesting crops, and eventually found steady work as a rock-crusher at Pacific Sand & Gravel. Perhaps it was this bone-aching work that awakened his business skills. Even though he was short on formal education, Joseph was long on common sense, and blessed with skills as a capitalist that would soon blossom.

While at Pacific Sand & Gravel, Joseph met the young woman who would become Hank's mother: Jenny Alva, daughter of Isabel and Antonio Alva. Born in Los Angeles on April 5, 1906, Jenny grew up in San Gabriel, and she and Joseph would raise their own family there. Jenny worked in a general-merchandise store, and the two met through family friends. Long after they were married, Joseph would break into song every so often, crooning the popular Harry Warren tune "I Met a Million-Dollar Baby (in a Five- and Ten-Cent Store)."

When Joseph, accompanied by a priest, went to the Alva home to ask for Jenny's hand in marriage, her parents were surprised; they had thought someone else had her heart. Not so: Joseph Aguirre and Jenny Alva were married in 1927 in the old San Gabriel Mission, which had been founded in 1771 by Father Juniper Serra. The couple would eventually have seven children in all: Fred, Helen, Henry (Hank), Irene, Joseph, Richard, and Linda.

Hank was born during the height of the Great Depression, on January 31, 1931. It was a terrible time. America's prosperity had suddenly ended with the stock-market crash of October 1929. Stock market losses for the years 1929 to 1931 were estimated at fifty billion dollars. The depression was a world-wide event. Companies failed, banks closed, and millions of able-bodied workers were thrown out of their jobs.

While still holding down his tough job at Pacific Sand & Gravel, Joseph Aguirre opened his first grocery store. It was a mom-and-pop operation, and, like most such stores, the entire family was counted on to help. Those children who were old enough to pitch in were assigned specific chores. Joseph was a benevolent taskmaster, but he was a taskmaster. He believed that hard work was a discipline that had to be applied rigorously. At the time, Hank did not totally agree with his father's philosophy.

Nonetheless, Joseph was extremely industrious and became self-taught in several ways: He taught himself to be a butcher, a baker, and a tailor. (He never made it to become a candlestick-maker.) Later on, he added the title of insurance broker to his many titles. The multiple business abilities of the elder Aguirre would eventually provide a comfortable and secure life for his family.

In all, Joseph owned three stores at different times, one in Azusa and two in San Gabriel. The family lived in the rear of the first San Gabriel store for quite some time. According to Hank's sister Irene, it was a difficult time personally as well as financially. Joseph came down with typhoid fever. The entire family lived in the back of the store then. Hank and his older brother, Fred, slept in a room about the size of a closet; and Joseph, Jenny, Helen, and Irene slept in the main room. It was cold and dreary, and all of them were all crammed into that small area.

Hank was a freshman in high school when his father expanded a business interest that was to have a direct and immediate effect on Hank's young life: Joseph made a heavy investment in a tortilla machine, and Hank and his brother Fred were assigned the chore of making tortillas for a developing restaurant trade. The tortilla factory was set up in the rear of the store. Space was tight.

All the orders had to be filled before Hank left for school—which meant that the two brothers had to get up before 5 AM and complete the daily tally before the schoolbus arrived at the corner. It was hard work. The ground raw kernels of corn were cooked into a mash in two huge kettles. The brothers would start by firing up the kettles and pouring hundred-pound sacks of ground corn into the boiling cauldrons, where it would be mixed with lime, to rid this corn slurry mixture—called *masas*—of impurities.

The boiling mash had to be stirred constantly with large wooden canoe-like paddles into a thick mash. The mash was then formed into *bolitas de masa*, or *tistales*, as they are called in Mexico, and placed on the bronze rollers of the tortilla machine, to be flattened and then die-cut into the familiar tortilla shape. A conveyor carried the tortillas into an oven, where they were baked. It was terribly hot work, laboring next to the ovens over the bubbling mixture of steaming corn and lime. In all, the two brothers' output of fresh tortillas was anywhere between sixty and eighty dozen! About a thousand fresh tortillas had to be boxed and ready for delivery each morning.

Add to the harshness of the chore the fact that Joseph accepted no excuses for anything less than a top-quality product—a standard Hank would learn to appreciate when he became a businessman himself years later. If the quality was unacceptable, Joseph didn't hesitate to hurl steaming *bolitas de masas* at one or both of his sons to remind them that the work ethic was the only true path to economic security. Excuses were simply not accepted.

Whenever Hank and Fred had a free moment, they'd race over to a parking lot near the store and play catch. Hank pitched to his brother hours on end, and Fred's hand would puff up and turn brick red, even with his catcher's mitt on— but Fred never said "That's enough." Joseph, on the other hand, felt: "That's too much." Usually when the brothers were playing catch, it meant the store was being neglected, so when Joseph discovered his two errant sons playing catch, he would grow extremely irritated.

One time Joseph caught them in the act, and the two boys ran to get back on the job, only to be intercepted by their father bursting out of the store—armed with a huge wheel of Longhorn cheese. He hoisted it high over his head and threw it at the pair. The wheel bounded past his astonished sons, almost hit some ladies who were walking down the sidewalk, and then bounced over the curb and rolled down the street. Hank and Fred had to pursue the cheese amid blaring horns, squealing brakes, and swerving cars.

When Fred was called into the military, Helen, Hank's oldest sister, was recruited to work in the store, although she did not get involved in the tortilla effort. Helen would be on the job at 7 AM, while her mother took care of the little ones at home. In addition to waiting on customers, Helen would make breakfast for her dad and then leave for school. Meanwhile, Hank was literally sweating it out, making tortillas.

To make life even more difficult, Hank's father decided to increase production and *built* a second tortilla machine by copying the machine he had purchased. Production doubled almost overnight. Joseph hired another hand to help out, but apparently the inexperienced new hire could not measure up to the absent brother Fred. Hank got a sharp taste of the irritation his dad felt when the help was late, or didn't show up at all. That help—as Hank described him, using a favorite term—was a "dunkey." Still, tiring as the work was, it didn't alter young Hank's blossoming social life, including his frequent all-nighters with his many friends.

According to all accounts, Hank was becoming a popular and attractive young man. He had many young ladies vying for his attention and did his best to charm them all. The family home was open to the Aguirre kid's friends and became a popular gathering spot for the neighborhood.

More than once, Joseph delighted that his early-rising son was ready for work at the required hour, when in fact Hank was simply changing clothes at dawn after a night out. Hank never let on that he had just arrived home, and instead stretched his arms as though he just crawled out of bed.

Starting with his grammar-school days, Hank had shown an interest in the great American pastime after discovering he could throw a baseball with speed and accuracy. All too often, when he was supposed to be minding the store, he was instead off in some field somewhere playing catch with his buddies. In pickup games, Hank was always the one selected first. One of the neighborhood rules was that Hank was not permitted to pitch—or he had to pitch for both teams to make the game even. His dad, however, believed that baseball was simply a big waste of time, especially if Hank was playing when he was supposed to be working. Ultimately, Joseph's resistance to his son's interest in baseball became a major sore point between the two.

One afternoon, Hank and a friend were playing catch behind the store. Hank's friend kept insisting that Hank throw the ball harder and harder. Hank reached way back and fired a steaming wild pitch that went right through the plate-glass window of an antique store across the street. Joseph heard the glass shatter and ran out of his store in time to see Hank and his friend take off at high speed. Hank even dropped his glove in the rush to flee.

His dad was furious. He picked up Hank's glove and shook it at the fast-disappearing figure of his son. When he turned away, Joseph spotted some trash burning in a wire incinerator in the alley. Without a second thought, he tossed the glove into the fire. Hank was devastated when he found out.

Hank attended and graduated from Mark Kepple High School in Alhambra. As late as his senior year, there was no indication that he would become a towering figure. Hank was then a skinny kid of about average height, with what he himself called "goofy feet." Although he tried out for the baseball team, he didn't make it—so he tried out for a cheerleader's spot, and won it hands-down. His fun-loving manner and outgoing personality made him a very popular cheerleader. "Fun-loving" was to be an adjective commonly applied to Hank throughout his life.

Eventually, as he grew to young manhood, Hank was pulled out of the tortilla operation and put in charge of his dad's neighboring liquor store. Hank was attending East Los Angeles Junior College by then. Between working at the store, going to college, and enjoying a busy social and athletic life, Hank was always in need of rest.

A bell rested on the store counter, and customers were expected to ring it when they wanted service, since the clerk might be stocking shelves or otherwise busy. Because the liquor store and grocery store adjoined one another (there was a doorway between the two), when a customer rang the bell in the liquor store, it could be heard next door. On more than one occasion, the bell rang insistently, and when Joseph came from behind his grocery counter to see why Hank wasn't responding, he would find his strapping young son lying sound asleep beneath the counter. There was always an appropriate consequence for an inappropriate action.

Joseph had no patience with Hank and baseball. But regardless of how dead-set he was against Hank's interest, the father was unable to discourage his son. According to a boyhood friend, Hank hung an old truck tire from the branch of a tree in a vacant neighborhood lot. Whenever he had a spare moment, he would lean on his buddy to shag the balls he tried to pitch through the tire. Hank was like a metronome, rhythmically developing his windup and delivery until he could put the ball through the tire, time and time again, from sixty feet away. Eventually, he was able to do it with the tire swinging from side to side, his buddy claimed.

Early in his budding career, Hank pitched for a local sandlot team called the Pasadena Yankees. One Sunday afternoon, the Yankees played a game in a Hispanic neighborhood, known locally as Madina Courts, in El Monte. It was an impoverished area, and a dirt road led to what was called *el campo*, where the ballpark was located. Early in the game, it became evident that Hank was in for a long afternoon, because as soon as he took the pitcher's mound, the hometown fans began jeering and taunting him in Spanish, perhaps not realizing that Hank was bilingual. The grinding tirade of personal insults was relentless. Hank's anger grew, and he slowly began to lose control—which could only have pleased the hecklers.

Finally, he wound up and let loose a fast ball that had all his anger behind it. The ball sizzled over the heads of the batter and the catcher, while the plate umpire jumped out of the line of fire. The pitch hit the backstop with such force that the screen exploded in a huge cloud of choking dust. The cloud ballooned out and drifted up, spreading over the infield and the stands. The ballpark grew immediately silent. The only sound heard was the creak of the rocking backstop, set into motion by the force of the pitch. Eyewitnesses reported that had the pitch struck the batter, he might have been crippled or killed.

When Hank strode to the batter's box shortly thereafter, the stands grew very quiet. They were especially attentive when Hank nailed a single into short center field and galloped down the first-base line. He was so wound up that he flew down the line, and when he rounded the bag, he tripped and tumbled, head over heels, in a cloud of dust.

The hometown fans cheered, then applauded, for Hank came up out of the dust with what was his trademark look: a broad smile. Standing on first base, he brushed himself off and with arms outstretched, yelled to his detractors: *"¡A un estoy aprendiendo a resbalar!"* (I'm just learning how to slide!) The surprised fans cracked up. He had won them over with his invincible spirit. There is no record of who won the game, but Hank had proved himself a winner.

At one point in his teens, Hank played Legion ball and pitched a no-hitter against a Bakersfield team. That ball became a prized keepsake, and he kept it in a special place in his bedroom. For some reason, Hank's younger brother Joe "borrowed" the ball for one of the many games the neighborhood kids played regularly. Somehow, that special no-hitter ball got lost. When Hank learned of it, he went on the prowl for Joe. Joe believes to this day that if their father had not intervened when Hank caught up with him, there would have been ugly consequences.

It was when he enrolled in East Los Angeles Junior College, though, that Hank got his first taste of organized baseball. He was starting to grow and fill out as well. In fact, it was the football coach who first became interested in Hank—because of his extreme accuracy and range in passing.

However, the baseball coach, Clarence "Ching" Duhn, recognized Hank's potential as a pitcher and convinced Hank to concentrate on baseball. Duhn was Hank's first real mentor, and Hank kept in touch with him until Duhn's death of a heart attack while still at the college. Duhn lived long enough, however, to see his pupil become an All-Star American League pitcher with the Detroit Tigers.

At East Los Angeles, Hank took business courses, and he also had a course in salesmanship. He was forever practicing his sales skills on anyone within earshot. A milk carton, lamp, cake of soap, tube of toothpaste—whatever was in reach became his product. He'd present the product with a great flourish, "selling" it to a family member, a friend, or anybody else nearby.

It was also at East Los Angeles Junior College where major-league scouts began to appear to watch Hank pitch. The scouts had apparently heard of him from his American Legion baseball days. Hank was eventually signed by the Cleveland organization in 1951. He was twenty years old. Tom Downey, a Cleveland Indians scout, visited the family one afternoon and sat with Hank and his father while they signed the papers for Hank's entrance into the big leagues.

It was a triumphant moment for Hank, for with the signing, Hank's dad put behind him forever his lack of interest in baseball and his scathing view of the game as a waste of time. Learning there was indeed a living to be earned in it, Joseph Aguirre became a believer, a supporter, and a follower of his son's baseball career from that point forward.

Chapter Three
From Cleveland to Cuba
(and Back Again)

Hank was a starter in the Cleveland Indians farm system through 1955, and he went back and forth between the minor leagues and the parent organization a few times before making it to the big leagues to stay. He had an impressive minor-league career. Hank won fourteen games for Bakersfield in 1952; eight for Peoria in 1953; fourteen for Reading in 1954; and he had an 11-9 record at Indianapolis in 1955.

A local sports reporter, describing Hank's performance for the Indians in a game against St. Paul, wrote: "Aguirre's masterful twirling advances his bid for earned run average in the American Association. He had plenty of stuff and mixed his deliveries well as he pitched his second consecutive shutout."

Another sports writer, reporting a game against Denver, observed: "Hank Aguirre and the Indianapolis pitching staff are virtually synonymous these days. When you think of one, you are automatically reminded of the other, for which there is sufficient and just cause. In 22 games [in the past three weeks] the Indianapolis staff has turned in only five full-route performances, and Aguirre has been responsible for four of them."

It was when Hank was moved to the Reading Indians that he met the girl who was to become his wife. Her name was Barbara Harter. They were a perfect match. Barbara was tall, willowy, and stunning. Hank and Barbara would be husband

and wife for thirty-five years, and it was Barbara who gave stability to the Aguirre family. Here's how that meeting took place:

I met Hank while I was still in high school. Oh, yeah! I was worldly-wise. I had never been out of Reading. Catholic schools all the way—grade school and high school. Hank was with the Reading Indians. He was twenty-four when he got to Reading, but he lied about his age. (That was grounds for divorce right there!) I was a senior in high school, and I saw major-league ball in Philadelphia before Hank ever did, because at that time, there were no major league clubs in California—maybe not even west of the Mississippi, for that matter. My grandfather was a baseball fan, and we'd also watch them on TV or listen on radio. I didn't know anything about the Reading Indians. I just thought they were a bunch of old guys who enjoyed playing baseball.

I had to take two buses to get to and from school, and I always stopped at the Picadilly restaurant in downtown Reading for a cherry coke and French fries while we waited for my second bus. Right across the street was the hotel where the Reading Indians stayed, and the players usually ate at "The Pick" before they went to the ballpark.

This one afternoon, a girlfriend and I were just leaving the restaurant to catch our bus, when she ran into a Reading player she knew. Hank was with this guy, so my friend introduced us and that's where it all started—on a street corner in Reading, Pennsylvania. After that, Hank began to give me tickets to his games, and we started dating between road trips. The schedule ended in early September, and by this time Hank had been to our home several times, so he was getting to know my parents and they were getting to know Hank.

On one of these visits, Hank told my mother that he wanted to take me to California to meet his family. Well! Major concern! Call the priest! And they did: He was one of my teachers in high school and would visit the family a couple of times a year. He came over and had a long talk with my parents. Everything had to be proper, you know. And the priest said: "You might just as well give Barbara permission to go, because she's going to do what she wants to do anyway."

When I look back on it, we were absolutely insane. The car belonged to a ballplayer friend of Hank, and it was a real junker. There were no headlights or brakes—I believe it was a Studebaker—and we started off in that thing headed for California, which was a million miles away. I was seventeen years old. We had no fear in those days. Nothing fazed us. Everything was going to be fine. And it was. Praise the Lord, we made it!

Hank's family was unaware that he was driving across country to introduce them to this young lady, so their arrival produced a great deal of tension in the household. Hank's father especially was extremely agitated because they were an unmarried couple, of strict Catholic upbringing, driving cross-country, and unchaperoned. At that time and given Barbara's youth, this was scandalous.

Our arrival changed everybody's life in the family. Hank's sister, Helen, gave up her bedroom, which was downstairs and as far as I could get from Hank's bedroom, which was upstairs in that big old house. The family was shocked. Hank's dad couldn't accept that I was a single girl, traveling alone with a man. It made no different that Hank was his own son.

His own daughters weren't permitted out of the house without a chaperone. He was very strict about that. Here I was, the same age as his daughter Irene, going across the country with someone I "hardly knew." It was outrageous— especially in the Hispanic community. Hank's mother saved us. She covered for us and would tell little white lies about where we'd been and who we had been with. I didn't feel I did anything wrong, but his was a different culture. I'm sure it changed all their lives because Hank was the first in the family to marry a non-Hispanic. I got engaged while I was there. It was on my eighteenth birthday. I called my dad and told him I'd received an engagement ring for my birthday. I'll never forget what he said when he heard the news: "You give that !@#$%#! ring back and come right home!"

We got married the next month—November 27— because there was no other way of seeing each other. Hank was going to Mexico to play winter ball. In those days, in winter ball, five American ballplayers were allowed to play on a Mexican team. The program was set up to improve skills. Hank was still a rookie and therefore could go to winter ball, make a few dollars, and work on whatever he wanted to work on. So, he left for winter ball and I returned to Pennsylvania, and our relationship was very long-distance. Here we were engaged, and we couldn't date or see one another. That was silly, so we decided to get married.

Hank flew in over the Thanksgiving holidays in 1954. My dad and mom planned the wedding. My dad and I talked to the priest at St. Paul's. We drove to Philadelphia to meet Hank's flight two days before the wedding. We rented a tuxedo for him, and he was so skinny that he needed a belt plus suspenders to hold his pants up. He had no rear end, and the pants kept falling down. Rocky Colavito and his wife, Carmen, were there. Rod Graver, a teammate of Hank's, was the best man. Following the wedding, we flew back to Mexico and winter baseball . . .

The Mexican team was called The Tomateros, and it was located in Culiacan. I was the only wife—or woman. Five American ballplayers, and I was the only female in the bunch. I had high-school Spanish, but I wasn't secure enough to stay behind when the team went on the road, so I got to see a lot of towns in Mexico! Barbara and all the ballplayers on the bus: It was fun! It wasn't the Ritz, but it was fun. Two things I remember were the heat and the dust. Many of the little towns we went into were so poor. Both Hank and I learned to appreciate the hope and the faith those people had. Life was pretty harsh.

And the local fans were intense! They brought handkerchiefs full of bees to the ballparks, and if their team was behind or they didn't like a play or call by the umpire, they'd flap those hankies, and bees would be everywhere! Here I am, eighteen years old, never away from home, in a strange country, couldn't speak the language, dodging bees, hungry for some familiar food—I wanted my mom! My father was right: Give him that !@#$%#! ring back and come home! I was so young, and so dumb. But I was also married, for better or for worse. I felt things could only get better.

The bus trips were awful. Many times we'd come to a washout in the road, and we'd drive onto a makeshift ferry—actually a raft made out of whatever was handy—and then we were pulled across to the other side by a burro hitched to a long rope . . . Life certainly wasn't dull. The people were so wonderful, and they sure loved *beisbol*.

The next winter season in Mexico . . . I was one sick little puppy. It was malaria, so they said, and the doctor ordered me home. So we left without finishing the winter schedule.

The third year of winter ball was wild. We lived in Havana, Cuba. It was touch-and-go because [President Fulgencio] Batista's government was in trouble. Very shaky. [Rebel leader Fidel] Castro was in the hills and was going to save the world. The place was overrun with the military, and it was "Shoot now, ask questions later."

The players and their families lived in walled and gated communities that were guarded around the clock. We weren't permitted to leave the compound because martial law was in effect. We couldn't go to a movie, we couldn't go shopping. People were being shot in movies and in elevators and on the streets. We learned to appreciate what we had in the United States.

Rumors flew! Castro was on his way. Batista had left the country. Foreigners were being deported. Foreigners were being rounded up. Scary times . . .

[Any] two or more people in a car were suspect. The military stopped Hank with five other ballplayers. He was the only one who could speak the language. Soldiers waving tommy-guns surrounded the car. Hank tried to explain they were American baseball players, but because of his fluency with the language, his story didn't fly right away. They thought he was a local. Perhaps it was because he was so cool that they finally believed him . . .

It was also in Cuba that I discovered I was pregnant. I made a Spanish omelet one morning. It was loaded with onions and other spicy stuff, and no sooner did it go down than it came right back up. So Rance, our first child, was in Havana during all that fuss. He wouldn't remember it, but he was there. I didn't realize at the time that we had so much fun. Baseball took us to many places, but Havana and Cuba were the most memorable.

By his own admission, in those minor-league days, Hank could throw forever. During his second year in the minors, he pitched all sixteen innings of a game against San Jose in the California League. He pitched thirteen complete games for Indianapolis in 1955. According to Hank, he was as strong at the end of a game as he was at the beginning. (He would prove his mettle conclusively in July of 1956, when he and the great Herb Score shut out the Baltimore Orioles in a double-header played at the Cleveland ballpark. The Indians swept the Orioles 3-0 and 4-0. It was a unique feat: Both young men were south-paws, and until they'd come on board, manager Al Lopez had never before had two left-handed starting pitchers on the roster.)

In the *Cleveland Plain Dealer,* sportswriter Harry Jones chronicled a story about Hank and Willie Mays involving a spring-training exhibition game between the New York Giants and the Indians—played in Wrigley Field, Los Angeles. (Yes, Wrigley Field, Los Angeles. At the time, the Cubs' Triple-A club was called the Los Angeles Angels, and they played in Wrigley Field, Los Angeles—a replica of Chicago's Wrigley Field, right down to the ivy walls.)

In that game, Willie Mays hit three home runs—two off Hal Newhouser and one off Bob Feller. Hank, then a rookie, was asked how he planned to pitch Mays, since he would be indeed be pitching to him the next afternoon. Hank replied that on the first pitch he'd knock Mays down. After that, he said, he didn't know what he'd do.

True to his word, when Hank faced Mays the next day, he knocked him down with the first pitch—also with the second pitch—and again with the third. Mays glared at Hank each time. But, being the gentleman he was, he trotted off to first base without incident. Then rookie Hank made the next batter hit into a double play, and followed that by retiring the next seven batters, to complete his day's effort.

When he was congratulated on stopping Mays, Hank tried to make it clear that he hadn't been throwing at him deliberately. He reminded his listeners that he had been told to pitch Willie high and tight—whereupon, he confessed, he got just a little *too* high and tight. (Hank's arm was, beyond any doubt, enormously powerful: In June of 1963, he would inadvertently break the arm of rookie outfielder Vic Davalillo with a wild pitch.) According to the *Plain Dealer,* the 23-year-old Californian was recognized that day as a pitcher with guts, and one whose reputation was becoming widespread. Hank was, the article said, "a nervy devil."

He demonstrated his nerve during a tight pennant race game between the Indians and the Boston Red Sox, when he was brought in for relief in the ninth inning. The batter he faced was the great Ted Williams himself—forever known as The Splendid Splinter—the last major-league player to hit over .400. (Williams would have a 1953 batting average of .407—after losing part of the season to service in the Korean War.). Hank admitted he was nervous: He was facing the best hitter in all baseball in his first real appearance as a big-league pitcher. In any event, though, he struck out Williams to win his first major-league game. "The rookie is tough," said Williams afterwards. "He's so tall and skinny, all I saw was arms and legs."

Another story arose from that game also—one that Hank told at almost all his public appearances in his later years. The story had become something of a tall tale by that time, but it always brought a laugh from the audience:

Hank was thrilled (he'd begin) that the first ever batter he faced as a major-league pitcher was the great Ted Williams . . . And he, a rookie, struck him out! He was so thrilled, in fact, that he screwed up his courage, marched into the Red Sox locker room, and asked Williams if he would autograph that strike-out ball. Ted obliged—happily, as Hank told it.

A few weeks later, Boston played in the Tribe's ballpark. Hank was called in. It was the bottom of the ninth, with the Cleveland Indians leading by one run. There were two outs, a runner on first, and who comes to bat? The Splendid Splinter, Ted Williams himself.

Hank burned one over the plate for a called strike. He waved off another fast ball and threw a screwball instead. *Strike two!* He then came back with a fast ball that was supposed to be low and inside. It wasn't.

Williams hit a soaring boomer over the right field fence. As he rounded first base, he looked over to Hank standing on the pitcher's mound—his head slumped and hands outstretched—and yelled: "Hey, kid! If you can find that one, I'll autograph it, too!"

Chapter Four
The Flying Tiger

Hank became a Detroit Tiger in early 1959 when the Cleveland Indians traded him, along with catcher Jim Hegan, for pitcher Hal Woodeshick and catcher Jay Porter. His career with the Tigers, and its aftermath, would have a lasting effect on the lives of many Hispanics who lived in the Detroit neighborhood called "Mexicantown," just a pop-up from Tiger Stadium.

Hank came to the Tigers as a reliever, but he became a starting pitcher in 1962. He was one of the game's premier relievers, but he was too good to keep in the bullpen. He proved he had starter quality when he chalked up, at 2.21, the lowest earned run average, or ERA, in the American League that year with a 16-6 record.

It was also while he was with the Tigers that Hank developed the lasting reputation of being the worst hitter in the history of baseball. Actually, he didn't deserve the onus—there were others with worse batting averages. Nonetheless, sports scribes had a field day with Hank's feeble hitting.

Throughout his career, Hank Aguirre was presented with trophies of bats with holes drilled through them. Of bases he never touched. Of electric fans. Of baseballs as big as soccer balls. It was during these early years with the Tigers that he was tagged with the nickname of "High Henry." I believe that Joe Falls, the premier sportswriter for the *Detroit News,* was responsible. Al Ackerman, a sportscaster for a Detroit TV station and one of Hank's staunchest supporters, in turn began referring to him as "The Tall Mexican."

Hank's worst-hitter legend grew exponentially. Ultimately, even when he hit a foul ball, he'd get a rousing response. A pop-up was good for a standing ovation.

In a game with the Yankees at Tiger Stadium, he hit a game-winning single into short right. It was his first time ever to bat right-handed. Mike Rourke drew an intentional walk from Hal Reniff, the Yankee pitcher, to get to Hank. Hank swung at the first pitch and connected for the hit.

The ballpark exploded with the pounding feet, hoots, screams, horns, and whistles of more than forty thousand berserk fans. It was absolute bedlam, and it went on forever. Hank's fans simply wouldn't let up. The game was stopped until they were satisfied. In those days, there was no doffing of hats, no taking a bow, no showboating. Hair was neatly trimmed, and there were no earrings, no gold chains dangling from the neck. The discipline of the great American game would not permit such unprofessional displays.

The fans demanded acknowledgment from Hank. He stood on first, one foot on the bag, his hands on his hips, and raised his beaming smile to the stands. As much as he may have wanted to, he couldn't acknowledge the rousing display except with that smile—and that prolonged the demonstration.

The Tall Mexican's lifetime batting average was .085. A few others were lower, despite the myth. For instance, his teammate Fred Gladding had a batting average of .016. Dean Chance had .066. When you consider that Hank spent most of his career as a reliever, his opportunities at bat were extremely rare, so he had a valid excuse. However, his notoriety as a poor hitter followed him until the day he died. In fact, his obituaries perpetuated his supposed lack of prowess at the plate. An Associated Press newswire item on his death included the following recapitulation of Hank's career: "Aguirre was also known for being one of the worst hitters. He batted .085 (33 for 388), with no home runs, and was two for 75 (.027) in 1962."

For a bit of trivia, however, Hank turned in a batting average of .500 with the Tigers in 1967 to lead the team in that area. You could look it up! Not only that, two years later in Chicago, he led the Cubs in batting with a .400 average. Fred Smith, the Detroit Tigers historian, brought those interesting statistics to my attention one day while we were talking about Hank.

Hank's baseball career was a source of lasting pride to the entire Aguirre clan. His youngest brother, Richard, recalled how their dad and Hank's older brother Fred would haunt the newsstands to get anything available on Hank—even his stats were of great significance. One of Richard's most cherished keepers was a Cleveland Indians uniform Hank gave him, along with a major-league baseball glove.

When Richard was a junior in high school, the Tigers came to California to play the Angels. Following the game, Hank arranged for Richard and a few other family members to fly back to Detroit on the Tigers' chartered jet. It was Richard's first flight ever. That, coupled with make-up of the passenger manifest, was truly overwhelming. Al Kaline was Richard's favorite major league idol, and there he was on the very same plane. Richard could reach out and *touch* him!

"Not only that," Richard said, "I visited with Hank for several days and rode to the ballpark with Hank and Al Kaline on game days."

As Hank and Barbara's own children arrived, Barbara had to adjust to a demanding way of life that ranged between that of a gypsy and that of a barnstormer. Playing ball was show business, and Barbara proved herself a dedicated trouper. There was a lot of picking up and rushing some place on short notice. She enjoyed the travel and meeting the great people. The kids thrived on the life in some ways and found it tough in others. Ultimately, Hank and Barbara had four children: Rance, Pamela, Robin, and Jill.

Jill recalled how, when her dad came home after the season was over, she and Robin asked him why he kept playing baseball when they wanted him to stay home. She also had the notion that every family traveled constantly, as they did. Every baseball family moved from town to town by private jet. You sat on Ferguson Jenkins' lap, and Ron Santo shared his peanuts with you, and Ernie Banks mussed up your hair. This was their life, and they thought it was everyone's. When Hank got out of the game, then the kids had to make a huge adjustment. No more Florida spring training. No more Arizona with the Cubs. No more special treatment.

That life was normal for ballplayers, but it was abnormal for raising kids. At that time, there were about five hundred big-league players in the entire United States, and the players were owned by the ball club. There were no free agents or the other liberal arrangements of today. Players were traded—or not traded—at the discretion of the owners.

Other kids in the Aguirre neighborhood had fathers who were home every night for dinner. They were at home on weekends. They were home when one of the kids got sick or had some other problem. A baseball player's kid had it different. Dad played 77 games out of town during a season. Dad might be home two weeks from now. If it was a night game, Dad wouldn't be home until after the kids were in bed. Then every player had "personal appearances" and the sports-banquet circuit to make.

All of this meant that raising the four Aguirre kids was left pretty much up to Barbara Aguirre. Other Tiger wives were in the same boat—Louise Kaline and Pat Freehan, for example. And yet as players' wives they too were celebrities, and were asked to volunteer their time for charity affairs—usually fund-raising efforts: holding auctions, running fashion shows, producing cookbooks, judging competitions.

One annual effort was a village community fair called "The Franklin Roundup." Franklin is a small community north of Detroit where the Aguirres, the Kalines, and the Freehans lived. The Roundup was held every year on Labor Day. Barbara, Louise, and Pat manned the "Hanko's Tacos" stand where they made and sold tacos to visitors. The neighborhood pitched in. It was a major effort, but a very popular booth. The Roundup was preceded by a parade, and Hank joined in, always wearing a colorful serape and a Mexican sombrero as he led a tiny burro carrying a "Hanko's Tacos" sign down the main street of the village. The stand did great business, but Hanko's deep fryers kept blowing out fuses and interrupting power, resurrecting the ancient, horrible pun: "Cold Today, Hot Tamale."

Even at the height of his popularity, Hank was a spiritually humble man. He believed that humility did not mean to think less of oneself, but to think of oneself *less.* He took little credit for the breaks he received in life. For example, he always said that his exceptional ability to pitch a baseball with speed and accuracy was God-given. Hank's own contribution, he'd say, was: "I took what I was blessed with and worked on it." And he did.

Hank's initial reception by Tiger fans was, in fact, less than overwhelming. He was little-known—certainly not a "name" player. Being a short reliever, he didn't get a lot of exposure on the mound. His first year he was 3-4. In 1959, he was 0-0. But the warmth of his personality and his disarming manner influenced people gently, and that influence spread in ever-expanding rings to affect more and more people.

The Detroit newspapers began to print stories about his humor, his way of keeping the ball club loose, but it wasn't until he became a starter that the fans and the city began to appreciate the new Tiger in town. And he was noticed for good reason: Hank came up with the lowest ERA in the league and was named to the All-Star team in his first year as a starting pitcher. Hank Aguirre had come into his own. Those years of playing catch with his brother Fred, of pitching a baseball through a truck tire swinging from a tree-branch, of Legion ball—all of it was paying off. Hank's father could not have been more proud.

Fellow Tiger Bill Freehan, who would later be Hank's business partner, recalled opening day at Tiger Stadium in 1964. There's always excitement on any opening day. On this one, Hank was the pitcher, while Freehan was catching. Tiger Stadium was bedecked with colorful bunting. Local dignitaries spoke, their voices echoing throughout the packed stadium. Team members were introduced to rousing cheers, which rose ever higher as the starting line-up took the field. Hank turned to face the lead-off batter, and Freehan saw that Hank was bursting with nervous energy. So, when Hank looked in for a sign, Freehan, trying to loosen his teammate up, gave him a fingers-crossed sign, meaning: "Here we go! Keep your fingers crossed, old buddy." That broke Hank's jitters. He stepped off the mound and a big smile crossed his face, and then Bill gave Hank the curveball sign to start the game.

According to Freehan, who caught Hank's pitches for five years, Hank's best throw on average was his screwball. A screwball looks like a fast ball, but comes in a bit slower than a fast ball—the batter is inclined to be out in front. Hank had a better-than-average high fast ball, an excellent curve, and a change-up that he used occasionally, depending upon who he was facing.

Interestingly enough, Bill pointed out, Hispanic pitchers historically seem to have excellent screwballs. Freehan named Fernando Valenzuela (a Mexican), Orlando Pena (from Cuba), Julio "Whiplash" Navarro (from Puerto Rico), Willy Hernandez, Aurelio Lopez . . . all excellent screwball pitchers.

When Hank came into the Tiger's starting rotation, he was third or fourth on the roster. Occasionally, he was called up in relief in certain game situations. But, in the main, Hank became a starting pitcher in 1962.

In Joe Reichler's *Baseball Encyclopedia,* Hank's stats for the big year of 1962 show 16 wins and 8 losses for a .677 pct. ERA: 2.21. Total games: 42. Total starts: 22. Complete games: 11. Innings pitched: 216. Hank gave up 162 hits, with 65 bases on balls and 156 strikeouts. He had two shutouts. He won four games in relief, lost two and had three saves. He had 75 at-bats, two hits, and no home runs, for a batting average of .027.

It was a beautiful launch into the big leagues, in more ways than one. Hank pointed out to me many times that a pitcher in the majors had the loneliest job in the world. "Could be fifty thousand people out there, Bob, and you're still all alone. Whatever it is—ball, strike, foul ball, hit, or home run—that's served up, you're gonna get a reaction. A big something's coming down from those stands—especially when all the marbles are riding on one pitch. Like if the bases are loaded and it's the bottom of the ninth, you got two guys out, the count is 3-2, and you're leading by one run. That's *lonely.*"

Hank loved a popular song, made famous by Frank Sinatra, called "That's Life." He was particularly whimsical about the lyrics:

> You're ridin' high in April,
> Shot down in May.

"That's me, Bob," he'd say. "When you're doing good, they love ya. When you're not doing so good—take a hike."

He would tell me that there were five stages in a baseball player's career. "There's no way you're gonna get around them, so don't even try. Stage One: 'Who is Hank Aguirre?' Stage Two: 'Let's try Hank Aguirre.' Stage Three: 'We need Hank Aguirre.' Stage Four: 'Let's try a younger Hank Aguirre.' And Stage Five: 'Who is Hank Aguirre?' It's as simple as that. [In 1962,] I just reached Stage Two"—he concluded with a huge smile—"and there might never be a Stage Three for me."

Tiger Stadium is located in the southwest area of Detroit, adjacent to the so-called Mexicantown, where the majority of the city's twenty-two thousand Hispanics live. The Tall Mexican endeared himself greatly to that community when he played ball there, and more so when he established Mexican Industries there. But from the start he also endeared himself to his teammates, acquaintances, and neighbors, regardless of their background.

Shortly after Hank was traded from the Cleveland Indians to the Detroit Tigers in 1959, he and Barbara bought a house in Dearborn Heights, a suburb a few miles southwest of Detroit. His new neighbor, Jerry Monley, recalls the first time he met the Tiger pitcher:

> Hank showed up at my back door with a big smile on his face and this kid in his arms and said, "I'm Hank Aguirre, and this is Rance" . . . That was the beginning. The beginning of a long and great relationship. Hank was one of the most down-to-earth guys you'll ever meet. Even when he became a millionaire, he was still a regular guy, and we hit it off from the beginning.
>
> My wife, Donna, and I had seven kids, and Hank and Barbara had three during the time we were neighbors. Jill was born when they lived in Franklin. So the kids grew up together . . .
>
> Donna and I socialized quite a bit with the Aguirres, and I enjoyed that. Hank was becoming a local celebrity, and it was nice to be a part of his popularity. We didn't have much money back then, and most of the socializing was done in Hank's basement with pizza and stuff. Every now and then, he'd get us tickets to a ballgame, but mostly the friendship grew in the Aguirre basement.
>
> Many times Hank would have a few of his teammates over—Norm Cash or Don Mosse or Jerry Lumpe—and he would invite Donna and me to join in the fun. Crazy times! We played with Rance's toys and giggled like a bunch of kids. Hank was the biggest kid of us all. He threw whiffle-

balls, almost broke his neck on Rance's pogo stick, and we tossed hassocks, ate tons of pizza, and drank lots of beer. Great times. I was sorry to see him move.

Jerry Monley is a talented artist, and Hank remembered him long after those early days: He called upon him many times when he started Mexican Industries. Jerry did most of his spectacular work simply out of friendship, but Hank found ways to balance things out.

Willie Horton, a Detroit Tiger star and one of the premier hitters in major-league baseball, was a rookie when Hank was in his prime. Here are his memories:

I first met Hank in spring training, and even though the focus was on prepping for the baseball season, they played a lot of golf, and rookies caddied for the big guys. That was the tradition. I was Hank's caddie. In fact, the only way I got on the golf course in spring training was to caddie for Hank. And Hank was a super guy.

Hank, up until the day he died, was the same person. He never changed. I was impressed with him throughout my life and my whole baseball career. Hank was more like a part of the family. He wasn't a stranger to anyone. He made you feel like you'd been part of him all your life . . . In my first year it was my first time being away from home, and Hank was one of the finest persons to help pick up my spirits.

Hank's dedication was evident in the many wonderful things he did inside and outside of baseball. He kept the Tiger Alumni together for many years, and some of the things he fought for are still with us today. He believed, *really* believed, in unity, and he brought it to the team. He brought it to his business as well. He was the lightning-rod. He spearheaded so many efforts for other people. Like how he fought for minorities in baseball management. Minorities in the front office.

He even tried to buy the Tigers. And if he would have done that, can you imagine what a difference he would have made? Under Hank's leadership, the Tiger organization would have been a model for all the clubs when it came to hiring minorities—especially Hispanics. That's how I learned to become a true professional—modeling myself after people like Hank Aguirre. He was there before I was. If you're smart, you pick someone to follow—and Hank was my pick. He was a great teacher in my life.

Reno Bertoia, a utility infielder for the Bengals and a teammate of Hank in the late 1950s and early 1960s, remembers Hank in a different way. Reno played in the big leagues for ten years, seven of those with Detroit. He was born in St. Vito Udine, Italy, and now lives in Windsor, Canada. He retired after thirty years of teaching history in Windsor.

I always remember Hank as being an outgoing guy—big, tall, gangly. When he pitched he was all arms and legs and a good fast ball . . . We sure had a great time. I put together a basketball team in the winter and Kaline would come over—I lived in Windsor—Billy Heoft came over, Hank came over, and we'd play exhibitions around Windsor. Then we started to branch out and we'd play in places like Grand Rapids, Muskegon. You know, big-time stuff. We even played in Iron Mountain.

It was a lot of fun and we made a few bucks—you gotta remember, we weren't making the money the players make today. We'd come home with a few bucks in our pocket and it was great! Hank kept us loose. He had a laugh in his voice that was just wonderful. He insisted, no matter what, things would get better. It turned out he was right, wasn't he?

I believe Hank saved my life, and I've told many people the story . . . It's a story men should hear: I went to Hank's funeral at Holy Redeemer, and two days later I had to go to my doctor for a six-month checkup. Just a regular checkup. And he's a baseball fan, so I told him about Hank's illness and the funeral and he said—right out of the blue—When's the last time you had a biopsy reading on your prostate?

I told him I guessed it was about five years.

He said, "Let's do a biopsy."

Mind you, if we hadn't been talking about Hank, this would never have come up. So, he did a biopsy and guess what? I had prostate cancer. Wow! If we hadn't been talking about Hank, I might never have found out about it in time. My PSAs [cancer tests] were showing, too. I will be always grateful to Hank for saving my life.

Ernie Harwell, dean of baseball's play-by-play radio announcers and the longtime Voice of the Tigers, is a pleasant guy who knows his craft like no other announcer. On a lazy summer afternoon, it was pure joy for a baseball fan to tune into a Tigers game, relax on a hammock in the backyard, and let Ernie's voice pull you right into the ballpark. He told me the story of Hank's only triple:

It was in Yankee Stadium and Fritz Peterson was the Yankee pitcher. It was somewhere in the late innings, and the Yankees were leading 2-0 with two men on base. The Yanks walked the next hitter to get to Hank—which happened quite often in Hank's career. So the bases are now loaded, and Hank saunters up to the plate. He's a little hot because of the walk to get to him.

Peterson's first pitch is a fast ball right down the pipe, and Hank said he didn't see it, but he swung at it and connected for a long fly ball over Joe Pepitone's head in center field for an honest-to-God triple. [It was customary for the opposition to pull in its outfield whenever Aguirre, as a "Hitless Wonder," came up to bat.]

Well, three runs score and the Tigers go ahead. Hank is now on third. I believe it was Tony Cuccinello who was the third-base coach. Anyway, Hank takes a long lead, then returns to the bag. Then another long lead—and returns. He notices that Peterson isn't paying much attention to him, so he turns to Cooch and says: "I think I can steal home."

Tony snatched off his cap and slammed it to the ground. Jammed his hands on his hips and spit fire. "Hank," he yelled, his nose shoved right up to Hank's face, "it took you twelve years to get here—don't screw it up now!'"

Ernie added that any man in the major leagues, especially in those days, deserves a lot of credit for simply getting there, because it means that he's the best there is. And any man who lasted as long as Hank did in the major leagues had to possess a lot of ability. "But as great as he was," Harwell added, "his [later] contributions to the community overshadowed his baseball career, because he was a guy who not only talked the game, he did whatever he said he'd do. He backed the words with actions. Most of us talk and don't do anything. Hank was different."

Mickey Lolich, a Tiger star during the 1960s, remembers an episode in the nation's capital when the Tigers were there to play the now-defunct Washington Senators. Mickey recalled a state of intense friction between manager Charlie Dressen and several veteran players. This discord was especially evident between Dressen and Hank. A great deal of the animosity supposedly stemmed from Dressen's belief that he was the guru of baseball—a man who knew all the answers and could teach everybody everything about the game. There were those on the team (Hank among them) who believed that Dressen got away with this style of management only by winnowing his roster down to young ballplayers—because his attitude worked with them, while the veterans saw through it. For example, Lolich said:

> Dressen got rid of Jim Bunning because he didn't like the fact that Jim threw sidearm. He criticized Bunning because Bunning didn't have a curveball. Bunning defended himself by saying he didn't need a curveball: "I throw fastball sliders, and I've won a hundred games with it."
>
> Dressen was immovable. "You don't throw a curveball, you're out of here."
>
> Bunning was gone the next season. He was traded to Philadelphia and won nineteen games his first season. Bunning is now a Hall of Famer. Dressen also traded Phil Regan to the Dodgers, where he had a 14-1 record his first year.
>
> Anyway, that's another story. We were in Washington for this game with the Senators, and Dressen was always on

Hank's case and he was out to get Hank anyway he could. It was our first night in town and the next day Dressen called a team meeting. He comes out of the office dressed in thermal underwear, sanitary socks and shower clogs . . . and Dressen stares right at Hank—never takes his eyes off him—and he says, "Last night, somebody was out after curfew and I"—his eyes are riveted on Hank—"know who."

He continued: "If that person does not admit that he was out after curfew. . ." And Dressen reached behind his back and pulled out a wad of bills—and there was a carpeted floor in the locker room—"It's not going to cost you *one* hundred dollars . . ." And he threw a hundred-dollar bill on the floor. His eyes never leave Hank. "It's not going to cost you *two* hundred dollars . . ." And he threw another hundred-dollar bill on the carpet. "It's not going to cost you *three* hundred dollars . . ." Down goes another hundred-dollar bill. "It's going to cost you . . . *five hundred dollars.*" And he added two more hundred-dollar bills to those on the floor.

"Now," he repeated, "If you don't admit—ADMIT—that you were out after curfew, I'm fining you FIVE HUNDRED DOLLARS!" And he's talking right at Hank. "Right here and now, whoever was out after curfew last night—I want you to raise your hand." There was absolute silence and nobody moved. Finally Hank's hand shot up in the air, and Dressen screamed, "I knew it was you!"

No sooner did the words come out of his mouth when one by one nearly the whole team raised their hands along with Hank. Dressen scooped up his money and stormed out of the room.

Mickey recalled that as a rookie just out of high school, he first met Hank at spring training in Lakeland at Henley Field, where the Tigers used to train. He remembered that Hank treated him well—even though, as he hastened to add, there's always a bit of uneasiness whenever a new pitcher comes on board because, when all the pleasantries are stripped away, it boils down to "This guy's here, and he's after my job."

It's there. You're a pitcher and a new pitcher comes in—a young one—and that kid is gunning for your job.

It's basic. Like the days of the Old West. You're a gunfighter, and if the other guy is better than you, you're going to be unemployed. It's that simple . . .

Rookies definitely kept their mouths shut. They stayed out of everybody's way. They sat in the corners and the veterans went about doing what they were going to do, and the rookies followed. You never jumped on the bus ahead of the veterans. They always got on first, and when they sat down, the rookies took whatever seats were left.

In 1963, I went to spring training and Hank had just come off a super year, and now he's super-friendly because he knew his job was secure and he didn't have to worry about me even though I had what I thought was a great spring training. I pitched eighteen innings without giving up a run. Hank was quick to give me moral support. He'd come in and pat me on the back and build me up and give me confidence and let me know what a great job I was doing. I appreciated that coming from a pitcher like Hank Aguirre. He was in his prime and was a veteran, and he took the time to give me a boost. Not may veterans did that then—especially if you were a candidate to replace the veteran.

Despite his fine record in the spring camp of 1963, Mickey was sent back to the minors. He believed two factors caused him to be sent down. First, he and Jim Campbell, then the Tigers' big boss, had some conflicts and, second, there were already three left-handers on the club. But fate intervened: When Frank Lary hurt his arm on opening day, Mickey was called up for thirty days to fill the vacancy.

Hank welcomed him back with open arms, Lolich remembers. *"Glad to see you, kid.* All that stuff. Pumping me up. Telling me how great I was going to be . . . He was just a big, jovial, warm guy who tried to fill you with confidence . . . I was in direct competition with him—but he was as gracious and helpful as anyone could be. That's how I remember Hank Aguirre."

Mickey's thirty days stretched to sixteen years, and he never looked back.

In all candor, he pointed out that even though Hank Aguirre was a left-handed pitcher in the major leagues, he was probably the most uncoordinated guy he knew in baseball:

> He couldn't hit worth a darn. He was not the world's greatest fielder. But he was a survivor. I know, as a player, we all felt that. Everybody liked Hank so much—loved his personality, his antics—that in 1968 we all felt Hank should have been on the World Series team.

In that spectacular 1968 World Series, Mickey turned in one of the all-time finest performances ever in a series competition. With Lolich on the mound, going the entire distance, the Tigers won the seventh game in the series (Lolich's third) by a score of 4-1. Every time Hank ran into Mickey from that point on, he'd put his arm around him and announce: "This guy should be in the Hall of Fame. He's no Kresge pitcher like me." (Kresge was a well-known "five- and ten-cent" discount store of the time, so a Kresge pitcher's win-loss record was in the "five-and-ten" category.)

Jim Northrup, another Detroit Tigers hero in the team's 1968 World Series against St. Louis—and one of Hank's best friends—reminisced:

> I met Hank in spring training in Lakeland. I was a rookie—a bonus kid just up from the minors. I didn't know the score at all. Hank was pitching batting practice, and a rookie is not supposed to make the veterans look bad.
>
> Anyway, I started to hit line drives off Hank, and the next thing I know, he wings one in and it hits me. I thought it was a wild pitch; but after one or two more line drives, here comes a fast ball right at my head. Later, Hank pulled me aside and allowed as how I wasn't afraid of standing in box.
>
> I said, "Should I be?"
>
> He replied, "You didn't even realize I was throwing at you, did you?"

I just shrugged my shoulders, and he informed me that a rookie doesn't hit line drives off a veteran in batting practice.

Hank was a real competitor, and at spring training we'd have these intra-team games where we'd divide up into "A" teams and "B" teams. You'd think we were playing for the World Series. Bob Swift was one of our managers at the time. I was up and Hank was the pitcher. The count was 3-0 and I looked over to Swifty, and he gave me the hit sign.

Hank threw one right down the middle, and I hit it over the fence. Hank screamed at me, all around the bases, for me to have the nerve to hit a 3-0 pitch. Sure enough, my next time at bat, Hank drilled me right between the shoulder blades and yapped at me all the way to first. On his next pitch, I stole second and he was still blowing steam. Eventually, he got me on a force at third, and he was still yelling at me when he stormed into the dugout.

I remember him well. Who wouldn't? He was one of my closest friends, and if you didn't like Hank Aguirre, there was nobody on this earth you could like, because he was just about the greatest guy in the world. He was helpful to everyone. He loved the game of baseball. He enjoyed life—and it was too short for him.

It was a sad day when he left us. Of course, we truly believe when we [the Detroit Tigers] won it all in 1968, Hank was very much a part of the '68 team [even though he'd been traded by that time] . . .

In 1967, with a month to go, four teams had identical records—it's never been duplicated in baseball. The White Sox, Red Sox, Minnesota, and Detroit had the same records, so every game that was played shuffled the standings. We went right down to the last game, and unfortunately we got rained out against the Angels and had to play back-to-back doubleheaders on a Saturday and Sunday.

We won the first game on Saturday and were leading 6-2 late in the second game and blew it 8-6. We won the first game on Sunday and had a 3-1 lead in the second game with McLain on the mound and if we won it, we tied with the Red Sox and forced a playoff. A pitcher who will remain nameless came in to relieve McLain and hung two curve balls to Don Mincher, and we lost the game, the pennant, and the chance to play in the World Series.

Very disappointing for our ball club. We had it and let it get away. I walked into the locker room and Podres, Sherry, and Hank were sitting in the corner, and they were all teary-eyed. I tried to ease their pain and said: "We did the best we could. We got our butts beat. We shouldn't have, but we'll get them next year."

Hank said, "I won't be here next year and neither will Johnny [Podres] or Larry [Sherry]."

He was right, and I always felt real bad about that for Hank, because he didn't have the opportunity and he had as much to do with the '68 bunch as anyone else. If you recall, Mayo Smith was the manager [then], and he thought he had to protect reliever Jon Warden, a young left-hander, and that was the end of Hank.

Warden's career in the major leagues, however, only lasted that one year, 1968.

Bill Freehan, a former Tiger catcher (and one of the best around), became a close friend of Hank as well as his eventual business associate. Bill tells, though, of a decidedly *un*businesslike incident involving a high-flying Hank and several other Tigers outside the Grand Hotel in Anaheim, California. It occurred one night when the Tigers were in town to play the Angels, near the end of the 1966 season. (That was an odd season that saw the Tigers change managers three times: The manager at the start of the year, Charlie Dressen, died; Bob Swift succeeded Dressen, but then he became seriously ill and was himself replaced by Frank Skaff.)

There was some sort of exhibit in the lobby of the Grand, and the exhibit spilled out onto the front lawn. Included in this exhibit was a P-40 World War II-vintage "Flying Tiger" fighter plane. Several of the Detroit Tigers, including Hank and Bill Freehan, got back to their hotel after a night on the town.

We decided—don't know who decided—but enough guys decided about 2 AM that we'd go out and fly the plane. It was one of those with the big teeth on the nose and those big fierce-looking eyes that seemed to glare at you.

Hank got into the cockpit, and the rest of us pushed it out of the hotel grounds onto what is now known as Freedman Street, and away we go. Here's Hank in the cockpit and about ten of us guys getting it up to speed. We get about three blocks from the hotel when here come the police—no sirens, just the spinning lights, the flashers. Well, we all take off . . . and Hank *can't get out of the cockpit.* He's got all six-and-a-half feet of himself stuck in the thing.

The guys that took off hustled back to the hotel, and we're looking out our windows watching this whole crazy scene. By now, the cops are trying to pry Hank out of the cockpit, and he's trying to explain that he didn't get where he was all by himself. Then he told these very considerate cops who he was—a Tiger ballplayer. With that, the cops decided they'd better contact Frank Skaff. Poor Frank. Here he is with one manager already gone, the other almost gone, and here comes the call from the police awakening him from a sound sleep . . .

Your phone rings at three in the morning and it's an unhappy cop calling to tell you one of your ballplayers is trying to fly a World War II fighter plane, without lights, down the boulevard, in front of the hotel . . .

If Frank wanted this whole episode to end quietly, he was advised, he needed to get some of the other players to help get the airplane back where it belonged. Frank began to round up some players, all of whom, when they were so rudely awakened, groused about having a sound sleep interrupted over some dumb stunt.

The crowning rejection was that about ten guys pushed the plane out there, but only a few of them owned up to having taken part . . . And Hank, God bless him, took most of the heat. Incidentally, when we pushed the plane back to the hotel, Hank was still trying to pry himself out of the cockpit.

Chapter Five
Human Chapstick

Hank was signed for one year by the Los Angeles Dodgers in the spring of 1968 in a trade with the Tigers for minor-league infielder Fred Moulder. Hank's role was to fill in for Don Sutton, who was just breaking into the majors and who had been sent down to the minors (Albuquerque), where he was being groomed for the big leagues. Sutton went on to Cooperstown after nineteen years in the majors. As a Dodger, Hank had a very respectable ERA of 0.69, appearing in 25 games. He pitched a total of 39 innings for the Dodgers and gave up 32 hits, 13 base on balls and had 25 strikeouts. Hank and Don Drysdale, otherwise known as the "Big D," became a pitching duo phenomenon. In 1968, Drysdale started a run of scoreless innings-pitched that eventually reached an astounding total of 58. As the scoreless innings mounted, Drysdale requested, and received, Hank as his number-one reliever.

It was Hank's superb relief appearances that helped Drysdale reach that astonishing string of scoreless innings. The string was eventually broken in a game against Philadelphia in June of 1968 on a sacrifice fly by Howie Bedell. The Dodgers still beat the Phillies, 5-3. Drysdale was elected to the Hall of Fame in 1984.

At the end of his one-year contract with the Dodgers, Hank was picked up by the Chicago Cubs in 1969 as a reliever. In two seasons with the Cubs, he pitched a total of 59 innings and didn't record a single loss; however, his baseball days were numbered, and it was his marvelous diplomatic skills that extended his stay with the Cubs.

Leo (The Lip) Durocher was then manager of the Chicago Cubs, and Durocher had engaged in a running battle with virtually all of his players throughout his managerial career. Durocher's biggest sin was his overwhelming desire to win. "Nice guys finish last" was Durocher's slogan, and he lived by it.

Leo Ernest Durocher piled up a total of forty-four years in the big leagues—seventeen as a player and the remainder as a manager. It was his years as a manager—where his testy personality and abrasiveness rubbed people the wrong way—that tagged him with the nickname of The Lip. Yet I watched him in spring training with the Cubs in Arizona, and if there was a child in the stands watching the workout, Durocher would always make it a point to walk over to the child and say something nice.

Phil Wrigley, owner of the Chicago Cubs, approved a precedent-setting position for Hank after Durocher dropped a hint to the front office. Hank's change from player to diplomat was recorded in detail in an article by David Anderson, a *New York Times* news service correspondent. Anderson referred to Durocher as a "human heirloom" who now had a mouthpiece to communicate with his players and newsmen: Hank Aguirre, "once a respected left-handed pitcher." The forty-year-old Aguirre had been appointed the Information and Services Coach, a position new not only to the Cubs but to all of organized baseball. The headline described Hank as "The Human Chapstick for Leo's Lippy Lip."

Hank Aguirre's easy manner and interpersonal skills were perfect for the job. "Leo always liked Hank," the article noted— even, according to a club official, when Hank was pitching bad, which was unusual for Leo.

It was Hank's new job to reach out to those who were reacting badly to Durocher's decisions and explain why Leo was doing what he was doing. For example (according to Hank), Durocher would put the lineup card on the wall of the dugout without explaining his choices. A player might be moved from fourth to seventh in the batting order for no apparent reason. When Durocher had been a member of the Gas House Gang, that's the way it was done.

("The Gas House Gang" was a nickname given to the old St. Louis Cardinals of the mid-1930s. They included Dizzy Dean, Ducky Medwick, Leo Durocher, Pepper Martin, and manager Frank Frisch. Originally, the Gashouse District was an area on the lower east side of Manhattan that housed a number of large gas tanks. It was a rough neighborhood. There are several versions of why the name was associated with the Cardinals, but according to Frank Frisch, the Cardinals had played Boston in the rain and traveled directly to New York after that. Their uniforms were very dirty—some were torn, because they were a sliding team—and the players didn't have time to get them cleaned or mended before the game with the Yankees. When they appeared on the field at the Polo Grounds, one reporter described them as "looking like the gang that loafs around the gas-house neighborhood.")

Players were used to a different style in those days, Aguirre explained. But the Gas House Gang kind of managing didn't work any more. Hank cited third baseman Ron Santo as an example: "Santo is an emotional kid. When you don't bat him fourth and no reason is given, he feels it. Slumptime, my friend."

Yet even though Hank was one of the nicest guys you'd ever want to meet, he understood Durocher's relentless drive to win, because of his own bitter memory of being traded the same year the Tigers won the World Series, 1968, and consequently not getting the coveted World Series ring that he wanted so badly.

Although Hank's burning desire was to wear a World Series ring, he might have settled for an All-Star ring for his 1962 All-

Star appearance with the American League, in which game he pitched three innings. But in 1962, the leagues had stopped awarding the rings because Yogi Berra had eight of them. "Life," said Hank, "can be cruel sometimes."

To add insult to injury, Hank was a relief pitcher with the Cubs the year they lost the pennant to the Mets, even though the Cubs had been 9½ games up in September. Kevin Collins, a former Mets and Tigers player, recalls that Hank had proclaimed to the world that if the Cubs didn't win the pennant that year, he would jump off the Wrigley Building and give the Chicago Tribune two days to draw a crowd.

Today, Kevin is a plant manager for Hank's company, Mexican Industries. In the summer of 1993, Hank learned that Kevin's business was faltering and called him to "come in and talk to me." Kevin showed up at Hank Aguirre's office wearing a three-piece suit. Hank had brought a couple of his management people in, and he promptly introduced Kevin as a new employee—because Hank had hired him on the spot. After the handshakes of welcome, Hank turned to Kevin and said, "Now take that suit off, you're here to work!"

Doc Silva, who was sports editor for the *Reading Eagle* when Hank played for the minor-league Reading Indians and who followed his subsequent career, did an excellent job of bringing baseball fans up to date on Hank and his role as Durocher's Chapstick:

> Area baseball fans are wondering how handsome Hank Aguirre is making out as Leo Durocher's liaison man with the Chicago Cubs. The going should be easy for the former Reading and major league pitcher since the Cubs have been moving along at a nice pace in the Eastern Division of the National League.
>
> Both Durocher and Aguirre are former American Leaguers, who have hit it off well since Hank moved over to the senior circuit after hurling for Cleveland and Detroit for thirteen years. When the lanky southpaw pitched for the

1954 Reading Indians and compiled a 14-6 record, he made a host of friends with his articulate approach to sports as well as non-sports subjects. Hank always was good for a yarn or two when he visited this department in the winter months after he became a big-league pitcher.

The suave Californian has been handling his chores as go-between for Durocher with the players, the press, and telecasters in fine style, according to what I read. . .

As a ballplayer, Hank was always interested in public relations. He always felt that baseball could do a better job of selling itself. To Hank, baseball is America's number-one sport, and he will tell one and all about how he feels about the game which brought him some wealth and a lot of recognition.

Silva noted that eighteen years had passed since Hank toiled for the Reading Indians, and that he hadn't changed much in all those years:

Instead of throwing sliders, sinkers, and fastballs at rival players, Hank has done a fine job of tossing a lot of nice-sounding words at his listeners. For a guy who won 75 games in the majors—mostly in relief roles—Aguirre is reported to be in his element visiting the clubhouse each day to get Leo's messages. The Cubs are for Hank 100 percent because he understands their problems and he is getting to understand Durocher better every day.

Following the unbelievable tailspin of the Cubs during the closing games of the 1969 season, Hank stopped by Tiger Stadium to visit some of his former teammates and to talk about why the Mets closed in on them. Joe Falls, Detroit's premier sportswriter, captured it all in one of his columns that September:

He looked the same as ever. Tall, tanned—with that bright smile on his face. He was wearing a blue shirt and seemed as trim as when he first joined the Tigers over a decade ago. But still—there seemed to be something different about him. Hank explained to the teammates seated around him that he must be jinxed and that he didn't think it was meant for him to make it to the World Series. He recapped the horrendous finish when, with a 9½ game lead, the Cubs collapsed down the stretch.

"The funny thing is," he said, "we kept looking back for the Cardinals." He shook his head, still smiling, and added, "We didn't pay much attention to the Mets and then, all of a sudden, they're on us and we couldn't seem to do anything about it."

Hank recalled that the worst moment was the night in New York after the Cubs had lost their second straight game to the Mets as well as a lead that seemed insurmountable. "I really felt sorry for Leo that night," Hank said. "The fans gave it to him—waving those hankies—55,000 of them waving hankies and singing to him the way they did. But it was worse after the game. When we came out to get on the bus, the fans were packed, against a wire fence and they were screaming at us—screaming and yelling every obscenity you could think of. I don't know why they acted that way. It wasn't the end of the world." Hank admitted that he had a decidedly different view of New Yorkers after that. . . .

Finally High Henry got up to go. His wife, Barbara, was waiting for him in the parking lot. He smiled one more time. "They can't blame me," he said. "I did my part. I hit .400 (2 for 5) this year."

Then he was gone.

Ferguson Jenkins, an incredibly successful pitcher for the Cubs, remembers Hank in some very positive ways. He had first met Hank in 1961 in Tiger Stadium, when Fergie participated in a *Detroit Free Press* high-school baseball tournament. He was seventeen years old at the time, and he still remembers Hank's warmth, great smile, and the cordiality he offered the players in that event. Fergie played first base and pitched one inning in the game.

A year later, Ferguson signed with Philadelphia. Four years after that, in 1966, he joined the Cubs in a trade following spring training. On joining the Cubs, he won twenty or more

games for six consecutive seasons, and when he was traded to
Texas, he posted a 25-12 year. He was inducted into the Hall of
Fame in Cooperstown in 1991. Hank, the pitching coach for
two of Fergie's final seasons with the Cubs, became Ferguson's
mentor. (As of this writing, Fergie is the pitching coach for the
Cubs. In the off-season he breeds, raises, and trains Appaloosa
quarter horses on a spread he owns in Oklahoma.)

Fergie and Hank got along from the very first. "We were
both athletes. We were big-league pitchers. So we had something in common right away, " he said. "He was easy to talk to,
and being a senior player, he had a lot of good things to say
about a lot of things. He knew the ins and outs of the clubhouse politics—and that's something you don't learn overnight.
We drew closer and closer. His son, Rance, would come to the
ballpark and we'd play catch, and that brought the families
into our relationship. It was nice."

Fergie praised the way Hank made the transition from player to liaison between Durocher and the team. He believed
Hank should have been an ambassador. As far as Ferguson was
concerned, he was. Ferguson marveled at the way Hank
soothed ruffled egos—both Leo's and the players' as well: "He
was the kind of guy that everybody wanted for a brother. He
simply got along with everybody. He even got along with Leo!
Nobody got along with Leo. Hank did. That's why he became
the buffer."

Ferguson explained that Leo was a controller who didn't
like the players to make any waves. In particular, Durocher
would have nothing to do with player reps. Marvin Miller, the
big man with the Baseball Players' Association, was anathema
to him, who wouldn't even let him into the clubhouse. (Miller
was instrumental in preventing the major league owners from
binding a player to a club for life. Determined to obtain
increases in players' salaries, Miller was a leader in labor relations for all major-league players.)

It was around this time that significant changes began to emerge. The reserve clause bound a player to one ball club unless he was traded, retired from the game, or was released by the club. This reserve clause came under fire when Curt Flood, a St. Louis veteran, balked at being traded to Philadelphia and brought the reserve clause under the intense light of scrutiny by challenging its legality, and thereby ushered in the dawn of the free agent. Baseball salaries began to skyrocket as a result, for it meant that players who went a year without a signed contract became free agents, and as such, could sell their talents to the highest bidder. Baseball salaries haven't been the same since.

For example, Hank, in his prime years, never earned more than $40,000. Today's starting pitchers sign for multi-million dollar salaries, plus bonuses to boot, which reminds me of an episode between Hank and Jim Campbell, then general manager of the Tigers. When salary time came around the year following Hank's All-Star performance, Hank didn't get any raise. He dickered with Campbell at length for an increase in salary and Campbell stood firm. Finally, wanting so desperately to announce that he did, in fact, get a raise, he went to Campbell again and requested "just a dollar raise" so he could truthfully say that he was given a raise for having had an outstanding year.

Hank had excellent listening skills, and the players trusted him. There were a bunch of younger players on the team at the time, and Leo scared them. They'd just freeze up trying to talk to the man, or their words would come out all wrong. If a player had a bad game, Leo was right in his face. There were no excuses. Hank, with his years of experience in the big leagues, could foresee clouds gathering, and he was able to detect those tiny wisps of trouble before they developed into thunderstorms.

"Many times," Ferguson said, "Hank took it upon himself to call a clubhouse meeting when he suspected there was trouble amiss, and when he spoke, what he had to say was extremely important to the guys. His advice had a lot of meaning."

The Cubs did their spring training at that time in Scottsdale, Arizona. One of the popular restaurants and watering holes for baseball players is a place known as the Pink Pony. Today, you'll find a ton of baseball memorabilia there that the proprietors, Charlie and Gwen Briley, have collected over the years. Charlie is an avid Cubs fan.

Hank and Fergie spent many a memorable hour there with the congenial hosts and many other celebrities. At the Pony, so many celebrities show up that nobody is a celebrity. If you sauntered into the place on any spring afternoon in those days, you'd be likely to find Billy Martin, Leo the Lip, perhaps Bobby Lemon or Ernie Banks. Mickey Mantle, for sure. The Splendid Splinter, Ted Williams. Dizzy Dean was a fixture. And, of course, you'd find Hank holding forth and Fergie having a steak and a beer.

If you visit there today, you'll also find dozens of caricatures of celebrities—mostly ballplayers—displayed behind the bar. Hanging on one wall is the first jersey that Charlie received from any player: It belonged to Ferguson Jenkins, who sent the shirt to Charlie when Fergie collected his 3,000th strikeout. You'll also find Hank's framed Detroit Tigers jersey, hanging over a booth along the restaurant's south wall.

Chapter Six
The Hunters and The Bear

Hank's baseball career came full circle in 1975, when he went back to the minor leagues. Only this time he was manager. The Oakland Athletics gave Hank the helm of the Tucson Toros, a Triple-A farm club based in Tucson, Arizona. Hank spent a year with the Toros and had a 72-74 season. That year ended nearly a quarter of a century of The Tall Mexican's participation in minor and major league baseball.

Hank had done well in baseball, and in turn Hank had brought credit to the great American pastime. Throughout his years in the game he had remained free of scandal, faced adversity with a smile, and seldom turned down a charity requesting his help. He now faced the challenge of establishing himself in a new career with his customary optimism. Still, there burned within him a fire to right the injustices and prejudice he perceived. When we'd talk about it, he would vow: "Someday, Bob, this is going to change."

What does a man do after spending most of his adult years as a professional athlete? He had been nineteen when he entered the sport, and he was forty-four when he left it. Now what? He had a family to support: a wife and four children, the oldest only eleven years old. There wasn't a lot of money in those days. He left the Toros because he simply needed to earn more.

Hank had an off-season job with a Detroit marketing firm, but his talents were not being used properly. The company failed to recognize Hank's many skills, and he was assigned to follow up obscure sales leads with the smallest of businesses. Hank predicted to me that the day would come when that company realized it let a good one get away. He went to work as a salesman for Lomax, a construction company based in Dearborn. Although he racked up sales, Lomax was having financial problems. So Hank was on the lookout for a change.

From the outside, you'd never suspect that all wasn't well. That same personality was there. The big smile, the aura of success. He still had a million fans who loved him. Letters piled up at his Franklin home. (Fan mail still comes in.) But gone were the up-front days in the warm sunshine of a summer afternoon in the old ballpark on Michigan Avenue, spanging the ball into catcher Bill Freehan's big glove.

Hank had a different calling now. It was a calling to help fellow Hispanics using his God-given talents and his developing leverage. I could see changes in him each time we met. He was becoming more introspective, more passionate about his goals, more determined to secure a solid base for his family and fellow Mexican Americans. To be sure, he sometimes felt the lash of prejudice, but he seldom complained. As a ballplayer, he had sometimes heard the jeers of "spick" and "dumb Mexican." Often, ironically, the slurs had come from hometown Tigers fans, who were looking for the crudest way to vent their petulance when a game wasn't going well or when Hank was having an off-day on the mound. But he never let that keep him from his objectives.

As an active member of the Tigers Alumni, he waged a constant battle to get more minorities into the upper levels of baseball management. He never raised his voice in anger. He was simply persistent. He never gave up. I have several of Hank's letters to Bud Selig, then acting commissioner of major-league baseball, and to others over the years, urging action on the hiring of Hispanics and seeking parity for the many Hispanic players in the big leagues who were denied access to the better jobs beyond their playing days. Here's an excerpt from a typical one. It was sent to Stephen Greenberg, deputy commissioner, in 1993:

> Dear Steve:
> . . . Regarding the issue of minority placements at the managerial and executive levels of the big leagues . . . I have never lost sight of the great vacuum that exists at these levels as far as Hispanics are concerned . . .
> With the threatened leverage of an opening-day boycott, it would appear the day of the hardball approach has arrived. You know all too well my feelings on this subject, and my letter to [then-commissioner] Vincent [Fay] is clear about the need for Hispanics at meaningful front-office, executive-level positions.
> There are many highly qualified former big-league players out there who would make excellent candidates . . . I believe, Steve, it is incumbent upon you and all others with influence in major-league baseball to pursue relentlessly the placement of Hispanics in the upper front-office jobs. Please feel free to call upon me to assist you in this effort whenever or wherever I can.

But it was the major-league club owners who made such decisions, and those decisions were not forthcoming then.

Fate had played some tricks on Hank during his baseball career, but it was about to present some major opportunities that, once seized and pursued, culminated in the formation of Mexican Industries.

One was the "minority-supplier" movement, which was just starting in the automotive industry. This was a concerted free-enterprise effort to make available venture capital to minority entrepreneurs to start up meritorious businesses. Another factor was Hank's acquaintance with Jack Masterson, vice president of purchasing for Volkswagen of America. A third factor was Hank's friendship with Bill Freehan, his former Tigers teammate, who owned a share of a manufacturing-representative company called Freehan-Bocci.

In all this, though, Hank was the prime mover. Without him, nothing would have moved forward.

Back in 1967, while Hank Aguirre was still a Tiger, Bill Freehan had bought a vacation home near Lewiston, Michigan, on East Twin Lake. One of his neighbors was a man by the name of Bob Slovinski, who was involved with a tool-cutting company. Slovinski and Freehan soon became friends. When Slovinski bought some hunting property in the vicinity, he invited Bill Freehan and his friends to hunt on the place. So Bill, from time to time, invited some of his baseball-playing buddies up for hunting. Among them were Tigers Mickey Stanley, Tom Tresh, Mickey Lolich, Al Kaline, Jim Northrup, and Hank.

At the same time, of course, Bob Slovinski invited his own friends up for the hunting as well. Among these friends was Jack Masterson, the vice-president of purchasing for Volkswagen of America, and a former purchasing director for GM.

According to Bill Freehan, most of the men he invited to the camp were genuine hunters. Hank, on the other hand, would put the orange suit on and prop a rifle on his arm, but he wasn't interested in shooting anything—except maybe the breeze. So when the guys weren't out tramping around in the woods, they sat around, playing cards, smoking cigars, telling a few bad jokes, having a few drinks, and getting to know one another.

It was during the years of these hunting ventures that the minority-supplier concept in the auto industry began to break on the horizon. So among the many subjects Hank and Jack discussed was the minority enterprise system—and the fact that Hank was of direct Hispanic descent. So the notion of Hank's becoming an entrepreneur came up from time to time as early as the 1960s. Nothing too serious, but the two men became friends, and a seed was planted.

A few years later, Hank invited Jack Masterson to join him at a baseball game at Tiger Stadium. This time, though, Hank was in a box seat instead of out on the playing field, and the talk was a bit more serious.

During the course of that conversation, they reached an agreement that would have far-reaching effect: The company would be located within sight of the Ambassador Bridge— meaning it would be located near Detroit's inner-city Hispanic community. Ultimately, the first home of Mexican Industries was on Bagley Avenue, just a pop-up from Tiger Stadium, in the vicinity of Mexicantown and Corktown—two old and colorful segments of southwest Detroit. The towers of the Ambassador Bridge were highly visible to the south.

"Mexicantown" is an Hispanic enclave of some 29,000 people within Detroit. Michigan itself has a statewide population of more than 200,000 Hispanics. This population has its basis in the annual migrations of crop followers, or *braceros*, such as Hank's father had been at one time in California. The *bracero* movement had gained particular momentum during World War II, when many able-bodied Americans were called away for military service, and legal migrants filled the country's critical labor shortage. The United States looked to the south for workers to pick the harvests of apples, cherries, lettuce, asparagus, and other crops.

After the various agricultural seasons were over, most workers returned to their homes in Mexico or Central America, but some remained behind, achieved U. S. citizenship, and moved to the larger cities of Michigan. Detroit's Mexicantown is a classic example. As the immigrants settled, married, had children, and filled churches and schools, their families created almost a city within a city. The community has its own newspaper, *El Central,* a weekly tabloid whose publisher, Dolores Sanchez, is a major booster of the city, providing leverage to move the Hispanic populace forward. The area has its own restaurants, shops, and small businesses, as well as celebrations that attract fun-seekers from all over. The community immediately became a labor pool from which Mexican Industries would draw, and it in turn has brought a measure of prosperity to the district.

Hank's company was incorporated in January 18, 1979. How it came to be is truly remarkable. Hank had talked frequently about putting together a minority enterprise. However, the actual formation of a company didn't get under way until three people came together: Hank; John Noonan, Hank's attorney; and John's wife, Mary.

John Noonan is roughly five-and-a-half feet tall and weighs well over two hundred pounds. His nickname is "Bear." Most people believe he got the name because he looks like a teddy bear. In fact, it started when a sports reporter applauded John's performance as a basketball player at St. Mary's High School of Lansing, and noted that "Noonan played like a bear." In John's junior year at St. Mary, his team won the state championship. The name stuck.

Hank and the Bear were both regular church attendees, contributing heavily to their places of worship. They became acquainted when their kids attended Holy Name School in Birmingham, a well-off community about a dozen miles north of Detroit. Hank and Barbara Aguirre, like John and Mary Noonan, tried hard to pass their strong religious convictions, disciplines, and values on to their children. The couples met at school and church functions, and gradually the Bear became Hank's legal representative. But unlike today's sports world—in which every aspiring athlete seems to have an agent—there was little interest then in representing sports figures. Athletes in those days, even stars in the baseball world, were paid meagerly by today's multimillion-dollar standards. There were few big contracts or endorsements, and certainly nothing else that required the full-time services of an attorney.

But the Bear and Hank's friendship grew, and, on rare occasions, Hank prevailed upon the Bear for legal advice—mostly in Hank's pursuit of a major-league managerial job. Hank had hoped to become a manager in the big leagues and took a shot at the Chicago Cubs, a team he loved dearly. When that fell by the wayside, the Bear helped Hank with the deal to manage the Tucson Toros, the farm team for the Oakland A's. So the Bear became Hank's lawyer—which, by Noonan's own admission, was no big thing. Hank had few legal needs and he didn't have any vast sums of money to brag about. After a year with the Toros, Hank had left professional baseball for good and was back in Detroit looking for a way to make an honest living.

According to Noonan, he and Hank got together now and then after working hours, and Hank would bring up the elusive minority-enterprise opportunity that was floating out there somewhere. Noonan listened but admittedly wasn't excited about the idea: It was 1976 and minority businesses were scarcely more than a concept. But Hank wouldn't let up. He was persistent. Hank's vision had to do with people helping others to help themselves. *That's* the dream he chased.

One evening in the winter of 1978, the Bear and his wife attended a charitable black-tie function in Detroit. On their way home, they stopped at the Excalibur, an upscale restaurant in Southfield, a sprawling Detroit suburb. Excalibur was a favorite spot for many professional athletes and other local celebrities. It was a Friday night, and among other notables Hank and Earl Wilson, another former Tigers pitcher, were sitting and talking. Mary joined them while her husband went visiting around the restaurant.

Hank locked onto his minority-enterprise theme and bent Mary's ear for a good hour or so on the merits of this humanitarian idea. He described the benefits the system would offer to the community, as well as the wisdom of hiring, training, and employing the disadvantaged. So impassioned was Hank's appeal that he convinced her on the spot. On the drive home,

Mary, a tiny, attractive, and determined woman, chided her husband for his apparent lack of interest in Hank's desire to start a minority company. In fact, she said, unless John made a definite move to form a company, Hank might get another lawyer. Which would be too bad, because Hank and the Bear were good friends, after all.

The following Monday, Noonan called his secretary into his office, and, over a cup of coffee, dictated the articles of incorporation, the bylaws, and the minutes of the meeting of the board—in short, he framed an entire incorporation document. When it was all prepared, the Bear called Hank and said, "You wanted a minority company, you got one. Get over here and sign these papers." Hank Aguirre was the incorporator and John Noonan the registered agent.

(How the Mexican Industries logo came to be is a story in itself. It took place in Bill Freehan's hunting place up north when Freehan, Jim Northrup, and Hank began doodling on paper napkins. After dozens of false starts, they came up with a logo close to the one the company still uses today. Hank took the rough sketch to a professional designer, and the only change made was the removal of a sombrero the three had drawn at the top of the "M." The professional suggested that the sombrero traditionally implied siestas and thus evoked cultural stereotypes of laziness, and so it was deleted from the original design. The rest of it, including the colors of red, green and black—those of the Mexican flag—remained.)

Noonan and Hank chuckled over the forming of Mexican Industries for years after that. It was simple and took about an hour to get done. The traditional image of corporate startups is one of heady decisions made around mahogany tables in richly appointed boardrooms, complete with the exchanging of signatures and huge sums of money moving through financial accounts. Not so with this company.

When Hank arrived at John's office to sign the papers, he didn't have the money handy to execute the procedure. There was a twenty-five-dollar franchise fee and a ten- or fifteen-dollar filing fee, so Hank borrowed the money from his friend the Bear. The company was capitalized with fifty-thousand shares of one-dollar stock. Nobody had ten cents in the deal when it was filed. John Noonan had fifty dollars at most invested.

After the filing, Hank received the charter from the State of Michigan, and asked John, "Now that we've got it, what do we do with this?" The Bear reminded Hank that it had been his idea in the first place; what did *he* have in mind? Well, Hank had a vague idea of starting a company whose true product was dependable labor. He had picked up the term *labor-intensive* from somewhere, and that was the gospel he began to preach. The big push at that time was for high-technology business. Labor meant hard work, and nobody seemed interested in hard work.

Except Hank Aguirre.

Chapter Seven
The Bridge to a New Beginning

Hank knew about hard work because his grandfather knew about hard work, his father knew about hard work, and he had been raised on hard work as a kid.

Hank also knew that there was an untapped labor force out there. A labor force that didn't exist, but that could be developed from the ranks of the people he loved: his fellow Hispanics. According to conventional wisdom, these people were unemployable: middle-aged women for the most part, with no way to get to work, possessing few (if any) marketable skills, and who spoke little or no English. Not much to start with and yet, everything to start with. Hank knew that, once trained in certain skills, this labor force could become self-sustaining. It was also Hank's intent also to encourage those who joined him to use Mexican Industries as a springboard to higher goals and more rewarding work.

Yet there was tremendous risk involved in starting a labor-intensive industry in the heart of Detroit, when most major U. S. corporations were looking to Asia or Central and South America for cheap labor. Only through the commitment of the American automotive industry did the minority-enterprise system make it in the car-manufacturing world.

Fate dealt out a strong hand of cards during the launch of the company. Before it even had a plant, Mexican Industries received a purchase order from Volkswagen Of America (VOA). For in fact Hank still needed a facility. The location had to be, as Hank insisted, "in the shadow of the Ambassador

Bridge." After some scouting around, Hank located a building on Bagley Street and decided this had to be the place. But he needed money simply to buy the building.

John (The Bear) Noonan introduced Hank to his banker, Don Dean. Hank and Don hit it off from the start. Don and his bank—Manufacturer's National Bank, now Comerica—believed in the minority-business concept. The result was a U. S. Small Business Administration-supported loan, backed by a $350,000 note on Hank and Barbara Aguirre's home as collateral. If anyone had doubted Hank's commitment before, that doubt vanished. With his house and most of his personal assets on the line, there was no turning back.

Bill Freehan and Jay Bocci invested their own money into Mexican Industries, as did Noonan, and Mexican Industries had three stockholders: Hank, the Bear, and Bill. Eventually, Hank would buy back all of Freehan's stock. He wanted to buy all of the Bear's stock, too, but John Noonan didn't want to sell. However, he did sell stock back to the company until his share was reduced to its present 1.6 percent of the total. Ultimately Noonan was the only stockholder in Mexican Industries outside the Aguirre family. Of course, as Noonan points out, "No one ever dreamed that 1.6 percent would become as valuable as it is."

The Bagley building was purchased, and the fulfillment of VOA's order lay ahead. But first came the building itself.

The first employees of the company were Hank's son, Rance, and one of his college classmates, Terry Henderson. On their first day of work, the two joined Hank in his old, rusted-out vehicle, and drove from the Aguirre home in Franklin to 1365 Bagley Street in Detroit. When they turned off Trumbull and stopped, Terry's first reaction on seeing the new home of Mexican Industries in Michigan was: "You've *got* to be kidding."

The building had previously housed a car dealer's "bump shop," where wrecked autos were repaired. Several smashed-up cars were still stored there, and the building was in worse shape than some of the cars. Windows were broken out. The roof both sagged and leaked. Paint dust, cobwebs, grime, grease and oil spatters, and indescribable ground-in crud coated the walls and floors. The rooms were filled with yellowed newspapers, mildewed magazines, old tires, broken headlights, and damaged bumpers, fenders, hoods, and rims.

Terry and Rance had the task of cleaning out, hosing down, and re-painting the place to make it tenantable. Hank's daughters Pamela and Robin were soon mustered to help out with the cleaning. Pam, Hank's oldest daughter, would eventually become the Chief Executive Officer (CEO) of Mexican Industries.

Enter William J. Flynn, purchasing director of Volkswagen of America. Jack Masterson, the vice president for purchasing at VOA, gave Flynn the responsibility for launching Mexican Industries into the minority auto-supplier business. Masterson's direction to Bill was: "Make it happen."

The first happening was the reworking of some parts that needed to be adapted to American cars. The first of the job orders from VOA consisted of sorting bolts and nuts. Crates full of them were shipped to the company from Germany. Quality control left something to be desired. The process called for eyeballing each bolt and nut, and tossing the good ones into one pile and the bad ones in another.

Hank's daughters Pam and Robin were among the sorters. Pam recalls the huge boxes in which the bolts and nuts were shipped. When the sisters could no longer reach them from the outside, they would climb *inside* the box to do the sorting. All a spectator would see were bolts and nuts flying out of the box to land on the floor in the appropriate pile. The good ones were packaged, coded, and readied for shipment.

The Aguirre kids, and Bill and Pat Freehan's kids—even Bill and Hank on weekends—bent to the task of meeting production schedules. Little by little, other jobs were acquired. There was nothing automated about the work. It consisted of tough, labor-intensive tasks such as the hand-cutting of hoses and of heavy rubber sound-deadening material. One job required some grinding and smoothing of fasteners, so Hank made his first major capital investment in machinery: He bought a grinder, on sale at Sears, for $29.95.

At its outset, Mexican Industries was a family affair, but Hank's vision of hiring Hispanic workers from the surrounding neighborhoods was gradually coming to pass. Outside the family, the first minority employees were two sisters, Pat Guerrero and Esther Jimenez—both still with the company at this writing. Another early employee was Irene Estrada, who, if she had been given an official job description, might have been called the odd-jobs expert.

When Irene started with the company, in August of 1982, there were 32 employees. Irene knew nothing about Hank Aguirre's baseball career; she simply heard there was a small plant called Mexican Industries down the road. Irene had recently been laid off from her job as a contract worker for the city of Detroit. Unemployed, and with an unemployed husband and two children to support, Irene had begun waitressing at a local eatery, but the family wasn't making it.

At that time, the manufacturing manager was Tom Kerr. Tom's key question in Irene's job interview was: "Can you start tonight?" Irene was unimpressed with what she saw, but in 1982, the economy was shaky and jobs weren't plentiful. Even so, her appraisal of the company in her first weeks was not too complimentary: No one seemed to be in charge, and she kept looking for "the system."

Then one day Irene saw "this big, tall guy come out into the shop." He looked, in her words, as if he had just walked in off the street. A fellow worker told Irene that the man—in sweat-stained work clothes and using salty language—was Hank Aguirre. The way he dressed, the way he talked, all his mannerisms, gave Irene a sinking feeling that the ship called *Mexican Industries* was being navigated by a deckhand. Irene concluded that the sheriff's padlocks might go on the bankrupt plant doors before sundown.

Irene's first job was sheeting sound-deadening material for a Volkswagen job. (Sheeting requires drawing a sheet of the material off a large roll across a table, then cutting it to the required length.) The job took some dexterity, and a lot of muscle, but very little of Irene's excellent mind. It was boring, tiresome, hot, itchy hand-labor, in a place she considered "a rat-trap." There were other odd jobs as well, none of them very stimulating. But the paychecks would make ends meet at home, Irene thought, until something better came along. Putting food on the family table was her only concern.

The lifesaver for both Mexican Industries and her—Irene now says—was a contract, brought in by Bill Freehan, for the company to make spare-tire covers for the GM Blazer. With that contract, the pace of work throughout the company quickened. And the employee learning process was simultaneous with the production process.

Irene was in command of the glue booth, a nook about ten feet wide and six feet deep. From a table stacked with round particle boards, Irene would pick a board, spray it with glue, and pass it along to a co-worker (often Hank's daughter Pam), who would slip the board into the tire cover, press it into the desired shape, and stack it. The fumes were sometimes overpowering and, unlike the air-conditioned plants of today, an open door was the only ventilation—even in the icy months typical of Detroit in winter. Production was agonizingly slow. Hank, Bill, and Jay Bocci worked weekends to meet Monday's production schedules.

With the spare-tire covers contract, Irene's job took on greater responsibility. The material for the job came in raw form–carpeting, vinyls, backing–and had to be quickly sheeted, die-cut, glued, boxed, and out the door. Proper tools were lacking. There was no established system or anything resembling organization. The process was slapdash at best, and the workers felt that it was Someone higher than Hank who guided them. Adding to the chaos was another parts contract from GM's Truck and Bus Division. Overnight, production shifted from make-work days to overtime, simply to meet the schedules.

People cut, sewed, and glued as trucks arrived, loaded, and departed. As fast as the parts came out of the glue booth, they were boxed and shipped–often before the glue had dried. Whatever was ready when a truck arrived–five, ten, fifteen pieces–was shipped. And the work grew, and grew, and grew. Even while the trucks were being loaded, parts were rushed through the system to make that shipment. There were times when everyone pitched in: the Aguirre family, the Bill Freehan family, Jay Bocci. There was little time to be given direction or to be told what to do. Each worker built up her own head of steam and ran with it. To Irene, it seemed a miracle the company met its schedules.

There had been no assurances prior to the tire-cover job that Mexican Industries would survive. But the temporary job that Irene took on in August of 1982 grew into a supervisory position in one of the company's most productive plants. Every one of those early employees was a pioneer. Look at their surnames: Guerrero, Castillo, Gutierrez, Hernandez, Torres, Medellin, Vargas, Aponte, Lopez, Garcia, Gonzalez, Velazquez . . . They were the essence of Hank's vision, which was slowly becoming a beautiful reality.

Whenever she looked around at her shabby work surroundings, Irene couldn't help but feel apprehensive. But as she witnessed the way the entire Mexican Industries "family"– Hank and Bill Freehan, the wives, and the kids–pitched in during the crises, plunging into the work with their hearts and minds and bodies, Irene began to believe that the company could make it.

Hank was everywhere and ever-present. When a press broke down or leaked oil, she'd see long legs sticking out from under the machine: That would be Hank Aguirre, ex-baseball star, lying on his back and doing repairs with makeshift tools. He operated the forklift, loading the waiting trucks. He rolled parts to the presses. He emptied the trash. Every employee could feel the urgency in Hank's presence, and at times they guided *him*. When Hank needed guidance, he never hesitated to ask for it from those on the plant floor. He never "outgrew" a willingness to listen to his workers.

In witnessing Hank's dedication to the people he worked with, gringos and Hispanics alike, Irene knew that she wanted to be with Mexican Industries for life:

> [Hank] was just as natural on the floor as anybody else. He never pulled rank on us. He was the same as us, and whatever it took—ten, fifteen hours a day to get it done—he did it. Got dirty. Did the gluing. Ran the press. Ran the office. Called on customers. Fixed the breakdowns. He did it all. He wasn't someone sitting in the office, pushing buttons. He was out there with us, right in the thick of things.

Yet however hard Hank worked, the late 1970s and early 1980s were simply not the best years for America's domestic auto suppliers. The founding of Mexican Industries happened to occur just as the entire auto industry went into one of its worst economic downturns. As a result, Freehan-Bocci was having difficulty successfully presenting Mexican Industries to its contacts at Ford. Hank was growing impatient, and the rest of the team was beginning to worry a little.

In 1981, Mexican Industries lost nearly $300,000. Business was in such a slump that Hank, Jay Bocci, and Bill Freehan met early one evening in Hank's office and discussed the possibility of dissolving the company. The entire industry was down.

Car lines requiring Mexican Industry parts weren't selling. Hank had been forced to ask for extensions on long-overdue bills to various vendors. However, grit and determination won out, and they decided they had worked too hard and had come too far to allow the company to die. Hank's house was on the line. Bill had invested a considerable amount of money, as had John Noonan.

And there appeared to be a rescue plan in the works. Jay Bocci had a contact with Dearborn Capital, a lending arm of the Ford Motor Company. Jay arranged a meeting with Capital to discuss borrowing money to keep the business afloat. Hank was excited and uplifted with the renewed hope that beckoned.

The much-anticipated meeting, however, did not go well. Dearborn Capital agreed to lend the needed money, but only on the condition that their personnel would then come in and "help Hank run the company." Hank wouldn't accept that, and bowed out gracefully, expressing his appreciation for Dearborn's interest. Mexican Industries was back to square one—broke, with a payroll to meet, contracts to satisfy, and overdue bills to pay.

However, Hank had two wonderful attributes going for him—an unquenchable spiritual faith, and dedication to his employees. He also believed, as his father had before him, that the United States of America was truly the land of opportunity. So, undaunted, the three of them decided to give it one more try. Hank, already deeply in debt, took out a second mortgage on his house; Bill, already in debt for money he had borrowed to buy stock, managed to come up with several thousand dollars more; Jay didn't have any money, so he borrowed from his father.

Now the company had new, but tenuous, borrowed hope—*literally* borrowed. As one employee told me of that time, "You couldn't believe how frightening it was." But everybody was praying and lighting candles at the neighborhood Holy

Redeemer, Most Holy Trinity, and St. Anne's churches. And slowly, piece by piece, sales call by sales call, business began to pick up again. Within six months, Mexican Industries was on the upswing. Work began to come in from all of the fabled "Big Three": Chrysler, Ford, and General Motors. Even the slightest breezes of prosperity felt good.

Chapter Eight
Green Cards, Green Lights, and Gringos

Mexican Industries was only one of many small firms that languished during the stagnant regional economy of that era. Another Michigan company called Textile Trim went out of business entirely, and Hank Aguirre hired three key members of Textile Trim's crew soon after the company sank. Each would become important in the development of the emerging Mexican Industries. One was an accomplished engineer by the name of Diane Brockmiller. Another was a talented woman named Gail Ward, who functioned as a sort of utility player—one of great competence and flexibility. Gail would lead, and train new employees for, Mexican Industries' sewing operation—a major responsibility, given the GM Blazer tire-cover contract. The sewing operation eventually became the backbone of the company's business. The third person was a manufacturing wizard, Tom Kerr, who had been managing a Textile Trim plant in Kingston, Ontario, Canada.

Bill Freehan and Tom knew one another well; Bill had sold Textile Trim leather-wrap steering wheels to Chrysler. Bill asked Tom if he would be interested in going to work for Mexican Industries. That day came shortly after Bill had arranged the major contract for Mexican Industries to supply spare-tire covers for the GM Blazer. Bill, Tom, and Hank met for lunch in Windsor, Ontario—Detroit's sister city on the Canadian side of the Detroit River. Over a cold Canadian lager, Hank invited Tom to join him in the venture. Tom agreed, and a handshake sealed the deal. Hank now had an experienced plant manager.

Tom soon learned that Mexican Industries was barely making its overhead expenses. Hank asked Tom to take a close look at the problem. So Tom sharpened his accounting pencil and discovered that, among other things, Hank was virtually giving Mexican Industries labor away. Overall, the company was earning about a twelve percent markup on sales, *if* everything went perfectly. If labor came out right on the estimate. If the material costs were on the mark. If there was no waste. If scrap was low. If the lights got turned off at night. If all these cost factors were precise, the company *might* show a little profit.

In Tom's view, at least a twenty percent markup on sales was necessary for any business. to stay in operation. Hank was operating on twelve; in short, at a loss. Twenty percent would cover overhead expenses, labor, variable costs, material, and so forth. The return is about nine percent. So Tom helped Hank to begin making the changes necessary for Mexican Industries to survive and grow.

In my communications work with Mexican Industries, I occasionally prepared green-card renewals—that is, paperwork needed by the U. S. government to permit non-citizens to work freely inside the United States. I would appear from time to time at the U. S. Immigration office in downtown Detroit to represent the company in this procedure. Renewing green cards is a tedious process requiring a great deal of reference-gathering. But the bureaucratic paperwork was a small burden to bear for the benefits that Mexican Industries—and the local economy—received in return. Many people might assume that, given its name, Mexican Industries' concerns about green cards were primarily south-of-the-border ones. And they were. But also among those green cards was one for Tom Kerr, a Canadian citizen and a key player in the company's future success.

It's my sense that Hank retained a trace of prejudice—or at least of insecurity and misgiving—in his soul. Hank Aguirre had dozens of good Anglo friends, but every now and then under stress he'd lash out at "those gringos" or "them gringo dunkeys" who didn't understand the situation or who were making his life difficult.

"Aw, you're a gringo dunkey, Copley," he'd occasionally say to me, jokingly but with a certain bite. (When I was growing up, it was considered disrespectful to call someone by his last name, so from time to time Hank would do it just to needle me.) The term *gringo*—a word used generally by Latin Americans to describe a North American or English man, and sometimes intended to be disparaging or offensive—has an interesting, ambiguous history. Linguists generally trace its origin to the Spanish word *griego*, meaning Greek. Just as English-speaking people commonly say "It's Greek to me," meaning that something sounds like gibberish, so *griego* reportedly was used by Spaniards and Spanish-speakers to describe a stranger speaking a foreign language. Its use in that sense may be hundreds of years old. Over time and in the Americas, language historians say, the term gradually altered to the easier-to-pronounce *gringo*, and evolved to refer specifically to U. S. natives and other English speakers. (The feminine form is, of course, *gringa.*)

Hank, however, had an alternative, folk-like explanation. "Ya know how you gringos got your name?" he'd bark. "From the U. S. troops invading Mexico when they were coming after Pancho Villa. They wore green uniforms, and they were one big pain, and the peasants let them know how much they wanted them there by yelling 'Green, go! Green, go!' "

Yet Hank always emphatically considered himself a proud American, and in business life he often spoke of the importance of "buying American" and of keeping the United States strong. Even if in his darker moments he muttered about gringos, he kept a broad perspective and understood that each individual has his or her own viewpoint to express, responsibilities to uphold, and a unique story to tell.

For example, his business acquaintance and friend Joe Schmidt, a onetime All-Pro linebacker for the Detroit Lions, recalls Hank talking in the early 1970s about starting up a minority company. But Joe didn't get the connection for a long time, because (as he later confessed to me) it didn't dawn on Joe that Hank was "a minority"; he never thought of him in that way. Joe also recalls their friend Earl Wilson joking, after Hank's business took off: "Back when we were playing ball, I was black. I've always been black. And Hank's always been Mexican. He's a Mexican. But look at him today. I'm still a black, but now that he's rich, he's a Spaniard!"

I think that Hank's drive, though, was based on something positive, not negative; it was a drive to help those whom he saw as needing help: struggling fellow Hispanics. Just as a rising tide lifts all boats, so economic prosperity should lift people, if they have been given an equal opportunity. Mexican Industries was a way to extend that freedom and offer at least the *opportunity* for advancement.

However, there was a down side even to the growing prosperity. As Mexican Industries business grew, neighborhood complaints were voiced. Letters began to arrive expressing unhappiness with the developing company's location. The volume of traffic, the potential danger to neighborhood schoolchildren, and an increase in noise all brought criticism and demands for the company to move. On top of that, some nuns from a nearby church began to picket on the street outside the company's offices, carrying signs condemning what they perceived to be unfairly low wages paid to Mexican Industries employees. The nuns clearly believed they were doing God's work—even though the workers at Mexican Industries themselves expressed little interest in the protests.

Visiting the plant one afternoon, Bill Freehan saw the picketing and asked Hank what was going on. Hank explained the situation, and asked Freehan to intercede. So Bill went out and tried to reason with the leader of the group. He pointed out the competitive nature of the auto business, the labor-intensive character of the work, the short margins under which Mexican Industries was working—and how there would be no jobs at all for neighborhood people if it weren't for the company.

"I tried," he said later, "to give these obviously dedicated nuns a crash course in the science of production . . . Explaining that Mexican Industries was not automated . . . that the company was just getting started . . . that we needed more time to get established."

But the nuns simply refused to listen. And with the neighborhood concerned about the safety of their kids given the increasing traffic, Hank was under tremendous pressure to vacate, with no place to go. At the height of all the friction, however, a plant site on Howard Street, only a few blocks away, became available. The address was 1616 Howard, and the towers of the Ambassador Bridge—so important to Hank—were still clearly visible. The move to the new location took place in December of 1983, and the building on Bagley was converted to storage use.

Business was still on the rise, and the company now had more than fifty employees. Mexican Industries' original work with Volkswagen had ended, and there was some business with GM and Chrysler, but Ford was now the company's major account. Most Mexican Industries employees were Hispanic, with some black workers, so that the workforce was more than ninety percent "minority"—and *minority* had become a buzz-word in the auto industry. Ford showed a genuine desire to offer projects that would help Mexican Industries grow, because the company so clearly expressed the spirit of the minority-supplier concept.

Accounts with Chrysler and General Motors didn't build up a head of steam until later, when Coyne & Associates came into the picture. Hank commissioned Coyne & Associates as a sales arm of Mexican Industries. The company was headed up by a former University of Detroit basketball star, Jerry Coyne. With his salesmanship and knowledge of the automotive business, Jerry began to open up new business for Mexican Industries. Freehan-Bocci continued as a Mexican Industries sales arm for Ford Motor's business.

Hank Aguirre and his company had weathered the worst. Now, Hank was increasingly seen not simply as a former ballplayer, but as a leader in the community. His standing slowly grew, gradually embracing the entire state of Michigan and even the nation. Articles about Hank and Mexican Industries began to appear: A small item in the *Wall Street Journal*. Another in *Fortune*. A short column or two in Crain's *Automotive News*. A brief feature in *The New York Times*. Closer to home, Joe Falls and Pete Waldmeir, two columnists for the Detroit metropolitan newspapers, *The Detroit News* and *Free Press*, were generous with their coverage of Hank's switch from baseball to business. Anthony Neeley, then a business writer for the *Detroit Free Press*, was particularly on top of the news about Mexican Industries.

Here was a charismatic businessman running a company with mostly minority employees. His firm was located in the inner city, even before politicians actually began enacting the idea of offering tax breaks as an incentive for businesses to move into "empowerment zones." Hank was giving a green light to equal opportunity long without its being legislated by the government.

But he was troubled by critics who questioned his motives. I know without question that he was driven to start a business in the inner city to create jobs for his fellow Hispanics. Here was a man, financially comfortable and widely recognized as a sports figure, who had the courage to stake his reputation and his personal property to establish a business in a city whose manufacturing base had vanished. His actions ran against all conventional wisdom: Industry forecasters were saying the future was in high technology and specialized skills, but Hank put his faith in unskilled people who were willing to be trained to perform tough, hands-on work.

But when his hard-earned success at last arrived, so did the detractors. Union organizers wanted in. Other small firms cried "favoritism." Still others diminished Hank's accomplishments, assuming that it had been easy for him because of his sports celebrity. When you rise above the crowd, hands reach up to pull you down.

Hank did become a wealthy man by most people's standards, but his true wealth rested in what he did for others. Father Don Worthy, a Catholic priest who today is chaplain at Saint Joseph's Hospital in Pontiac, tells of one such occasion. He was then serving as chaplain at the old Mount Carmel Hospital, on Detroit's west side. Father Worthy had counseled a woman there during several previous visits, and now she was in the last stages of renal failure. In the course of their last conversation, the woman told Father Worthy of her two teenage sons, who were attending Aquinas High School in Southgate, Michigan. She was a single parent, and the chaplain asked how—ill as she clearly was and had been—she still could afford to send two children to such a good school.

Her boss had told her, she replied, that when she was no longer able to work, she would never need to worry about the education of her sons—he would take care of their tuition. When Father Worthy asked who this man was, the woman told him that her benefactor had strictly told her never to disclose his name; but since she was so close to death, and so grateful, she revealed that it was Hank Aguirre.

Father Worthy told me he had never forgotten that conversation: Here was a former Detroit Tiger who elected to stick with the city, after his baseball career had ended. Here was a man who didn't take the money and run, but whose words of goodwill were backed by action, and who had no intention of following the corporate exodus out of Detroit.

Even back in 1979, in its first year in business, Mexican Industries sales had managed to round out at about $314,000— roughly the amount of the original loan. Hank didn't draw a salary. And he kept the sales figures in a spiral-bound note book, which he carried around in his hip pocket. Each week, Hank tallied up the production and sales figures; if the numbers were in the black, the staff would meet to celebrate at The Hummer, a sports bar-and-grill across the street from the Bagley plant. Years later, family members and friends searched through family memorabilia—in cupboards, closets, basements, and the like—trying to find this earliest record of the company's books, but to no avail.

Hank Aguirre, age 3, with his future best friend.

The Aguirre family. Hank stands behind the couch, at right.
Clockwise: Hank; his mother, Jenny, with sister Linda in her lap;
sister Irene; brother Richard, in lap of sister Helen; brothers Joseph
and Fred; and at center Hank's father, Joseph.

The young worker, in front of the Aguirre family store
in San Gabriel, California. The sign reads:
CORN TORTILLAS FOR SALE HERE.

A proud high-school graduate, 1949. Hank completed both high school and junior college before embarking on a baseball career.

The brash rookie, grinning like the Cleveland Indian emblazoned on his cap and uniform, 1953.

Pitching star for the Detroit Tigers.
Hank's lifetime ERA was 3.24.

In his All-Star Year of 1962, Hank simultaneously accepts from the Detroit Baseball Writers Association both a plaque for pitching excellence and the group's "Horrible Hitter Award."

Tagged out during an exhibition game in Tokyo, Japan, 1962.

In the dugout with Gov. George Romney (R-Michigan) on Opening
Day, 1965. In the wake of Detroit's urban riots in the summer of
1967, Romney—an ardent advocate of volunteerism—would go on to
serve as U. S. Secretary of Housing and Urban Development. As a
businessman, Hank would privately serve his community and work
for urban renewal in Detroit.

Rance Aguirre pitches a curveball to a nervous batter at a Tiger
Stadium father-son game, 1966.

The Aguirre family in Lakeland, Florida,
for Hank's spring training in 1967.
From left to right: Pam, Barbara, Rance, Robin, Hank, and Jill.

Towering over the Giant:
The Tall Mexican, Los Angeles Dodger Hank Aguirre, with Willie
Mays of the San Francisco Giants, 1969.

Two Hanks and a Banks:
Atlanta Brave Hank Aaron and Chicago Cubs Hank Aguirre and
Ernie Banks, at Wrigley Field. All told, the three men racked up
more than 1,200 home runs.

Coach Aguirre of the Chicago Cubs offers pitching tips to a rookie
during spring training.

The manager of the Tucson Toros in a pensive mood. This would
be Aguirre's last year in pro baseball. He would soon bravely
embark upon a new career.

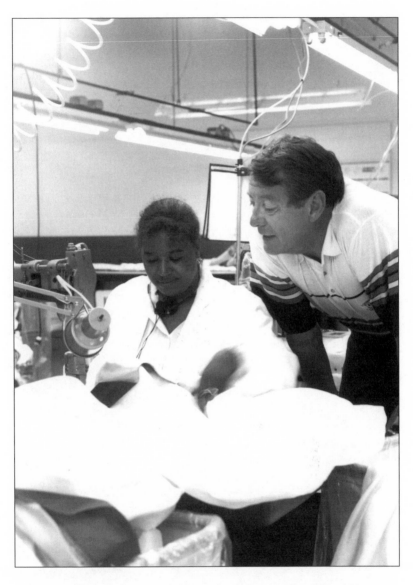

On the main floor of the Howard plant, Hank talks with a Mexican Industries worker at her sewing machine. Others credited a good share of Hank's success as a businessman to his caring attitude towards his employees.

The proud CEO of Mexican Industries,
with his "Man of the Year" Award from the
U. S. Hispanic Chamber of Commerce, in 1990.

Chapter Nine
Cave Drawings

Today, the site of the corporate headquarters of Mexican Industries, called Aguirre Plaza, stands at the corner of Howard Street and Rosa Parks (named after the black civil-rights heroine). It is even closer to the Ambassador Bridge—so important to Hank—than the Bagley plant was. At night, the necklace of lights running along the bridge's suspension cables is visible from every office on Aguirre Plaza's south side. The plaza building is surrounded by an expanse of lush green lawn, dotted by trees.

At the time when Hank selected this site, though, the area surrounding the current plant locations had been given up for dead. He planted his banner and determined to improve what was seen as hopeless.

Another famous Detroit landmark, visible from the plaza, indicates the deterioration into which the area had sunk. Looming above the horizon southwest of Aguirre Plaza are the skeletal remains of a once grand landmark building, the Michigan Central Railroad Station. Nearly every window of this formerly bustling terminal has been smashed. Weeds grow up through cracks in the broken concrete walks leading to the great entrance. The heavy bronze revolving doors that once graced that entrance are gone. Inside, illegible graffiti and obscenities have been spray-painted on the floor and the stately columns of the lobby. The interior is trashed. Beautiful marble slabs have been ripped out. If you are inclined to whistle, the sound bounces off the bare walls, and on windswept days an audible moan resonates through the ruins.

To the east of Aguirre Plaza stands the burned-out hulk of a seven-story, red-brick building that once housed a tire distribution company. When that company moved out, the building became a warehouse, then a vacant relic that went up in flames some years back. The roof is gone, and charred timbers criss-cross a jumble of debris. Vandals have probably been the only visitors to the place since firefighters departed. Meanwhile, across Rosa Parks are decaying warehouses and storefronts that have been boarded up for more than a decade. And to the west is a former church building whose congregation has moved elsewhere. Everywhere there is gang graffiti.

Yet this is the center of operations for Mexican Industries. Four manufacturing sites and the corporate headquarters now stand there, a productive, pleasant, and green-lawned haven where urban blight and indifference had once entirely drained the area of its lifeblood.

When Bill Flynn, purchasing chief for Volkswagen of America and a business friend of Hank, decided to take early retirement, Hank asked Bill to join Mexican Industries in a similar capacity. Both men had a great deal of respect for each other, and Bill's hiring proved an excellent match. Along with many other responsibilities, Bill Flynn became a key figure in overseeing the construction of those new corporate headquarters. A trim man with a great smile and an approachable manner, Bill Flynn has a youthful, ruddy face that belies his white hair and years of experience. His startling blue eyes show a quiet sense of humor that has eased Mexican Industries through many difficult and stressful times.

And Hank's impatience over the progress of the construction of Aguirre Plaza was visited many times on Bill Flynn. (The planning of the new corporate headquarters was such a massive project that groundbreaking ceremonies did not take place until November of 1993.) Bill worked quietly, often arranging tasks that seemed impossible to accomplish.

However, when Hank received a progress report that didn't suit him, he'd dress Bill down sharply, and when Hank was wound up, his salty vocabulary could become blistering. (He also had a habit, during such outbursts, of rubbing his forehead with thumb and index finger until his skin blushed red.) But Bill was imperturbable, and would silently listen, then defuse the situation softly. For his part, Hank never let his exasperation linger once an eruption was done. "Let's move on" was his usual blowout-ending remark. Everyone in the room looked forward to those words. (Bill Flynn especially.)

Hank's sting, however, could also take more charming forms. He enjoyed verbal sparring. He could bait you and keep you on the defensive, and he loved the give-and-take of a conversational scuffle. I've said before that Hank understood the power of words. I wrote all his speeches at his many public appearances, and generally we'd sit down a few weeks ahead of the speaking engagement, at which time he'd give me the message he wished to convey and the general direction he wanted to take. I knew him so well, and had worked with him so often, that my texts usually came pretty close to the bullseye. But sometimes Hank delighted in needling me over the best way to employ those words.

"You're so smart, Bob," he'd say, handing me a pencil. "Sell this pencil to me."

I would go along, knowing that whatever I came up with wouldn't be right: "The bright yellow color makes it easy to find. The eraser doesn't smear. The lead is made of the best graphite."

"Naw. Get with it," he'd say. "That's not how to do it! You don't sell *it*, you sell what it can *do!*"

"What it can do?"

"You should know, you're the writer."

I'd play along: "With it you can ask questions?"

"You're getting warm . . . *gringo*," he'd say, toying with me with an innocent look and a disarming smile. Then he'd lay it on me: "You can *communicate!* With a pencil, my friend, you can make love, keep somebody's telephone number, draw a picture, keep a diary—all kinds of things! You can leave your *mark* behind you. After all, what about those cave drawings?"

"Cave drawings?"

"Those cave drawings. What if those cave people hadn't had something to draw with? We would have never known they were there."

Even when he goaded and occasionally bullied them, Hank always showed an uncommon feeling for people, and he surrounded himself with workers who gave Mexican Industries the best support they could.

Hank's friend Joe Schmidt, as a former All-Pro linebacker for the Detroit Lions now in the Football Hall of Fame, had something to say on this subject. (Hank was, incidentally, one of the few baseball players who socialized with football players.) Joe, who coached the Lions for six seasons following his retirement as a player, commented to me that most professional athletes become very intuitive about people: They can pick the good guys out of a crowd in a short time.

The character of those in pro sports, he suggested, comes to the surface quickly, because such athletes must perform under tremendous physical and mental duress, and their performance is measured before thousands of people. "Flaws," he noted, "show up under that heavy glare." Former athletes like Hank Aguirre who enter the business world, he argued, bring with them the ability to perform under fire, and have acquired an intuitive sense to surround themselves with people capable of performing equally well. When I recall the key people he hired to help him move Mexican Industries forward, I believe that was true of Hank.

By the end of the fiscal year in June 1984, the company reported $8.4 million in sales and 84 employees. In August,

John Livingstone joined Mexican Industries as its first comptroller. (Before John's arrival, day-to-day accounting had been handled by company people, but an outside accounting firm had closed the books each month.) Hank figured he would do better and save money by handling the accounting in-house, and John had a deep appreciation and understanding of the minority-supplier concept.

By September of 1984, Mexican Industries had a hundred employees and annual sales had reached close to $8.5 million. The Howard Street plant was fully occupied. Jerry Coyne of Coyne and Associates began representing Mexican Industries at Chrysler. Although Chrysler didn't have a strong minority program, Jerry persisted and eventually got a small contract for Mexican Industries. It wasn't great, but it was a start.

When Chrysler decided to farm out a major package that had been produced internally, Jerry's persistence paid off. He brought the assembly job to Mexican Industries, and it launched a long-term business relationship with Chrysler. Sales slowly rose from zero to a million, to ten million, to twenty million, to the present thirty million dollars in direct sales alone. (Chrysler-related business by the 1990s would total around fifty million dollars.)

In 1985, Mexican Industries was given the opportunity by Ford to quote on two separate jobs: an emergency-equipment tool kit for the 1986 Taurus, and a contract for convenience nets—those tie-down nets that prevent cargo from shifting in the trunk of a car or back of a station wagon. The awarding of the convenience-net contract from Ford Purchasing was a like a gift. Those two products accounted for most of the cash flow for Mexican Industries for years, and were the most profitable products in the company's line. And as a minority supplier, Mexican Industries was given favorable terms of business, allowing the company to generate interest on incoming money before paying off its own suppliers. For years, therefore, Mexican Industries never needed to borrow money against its line of credit. The cash generated bought all the company's computer equipment, and allowed Hank to provide increased benefits for his employees.

Those workers—not Aguirre Plaza, however beautiful it became—were the heart of Hank's company.

Hank had his own personality quirks. He allowed only certain people to get close to him, and some business associates described him as "an island." Attending Mass with him, I learned early on that Hank didn't like to hold hands during recital of the "Our Father." To those giving him the occasional hug, it could be like hugging an ironing board. But when Hank was in the company of his employees at a company function, he didn't hesitate to embrace the women he called "his ladies." He welcomed employees who appeared at his office seeking counsel or help.

One of Hank's "ladies" was Gracie Zuniga, a beautiful woman with steel-gray hair and dark, penetrating eyes. She came to the United States from Tampico in 1947.

> I remember Hank when he played for the Tigers. I lived close by the stadium. We were all crazy about him because he was Mexican and all the girls go to talk to him. We all thought he was so good-looking, and he was my age and he spoke Spanish, so my sister and me and all the girls would go see him. The lines were so long and we waited and waited just to see him and say hello. I have good, good memories of him. . .
> He had a beautiful heart. He took care of his people. Any problem. He fixed it . . . He gave so many people the chance to work. He would come by and put his hand in your arm and talk to you and you feel good. He was the same way with everybody. He made you feel happy.

Gracie had left her previous job as a beautician after fifteen years because she was unable to tolerate the long hours spent standing. She was a skilled seamstress as well, so it seemed natural for her to gravitate to Mexican Industries, where she could work sitting down at a sewing machine:

> I was afraid [to apply for work at Mexican Industries], because at this time I'm old already, you know, and I said, Maybe they can't take me because I'm fifty-something. And I told Hank I'm fifty-something, you don't mind? He told me I was a good soul and he didn't care about my age. And I come and take a test and I pass—never worked in a company for sewing, but I sew at home, you know, so it wasn't too hard to learn what they wanted me to do at Mexican Industries. I was working the same day I was hired.
>
> Later Hank wanted me to work in quality control and then be a line leader. He wanted me to move up, but I had to have a job where I could sit . . . Hank wanted the best for me. That's why he wanted me to be a supervisor. Not only me, he wanted what was best for everybody.

At times she would pass by Hank's office, and Hank would see her and ask her in, regardless of what was going on or who was in the office. He would see her, wave for her to come in, and he would give her a kiss and touch her hand, while Gracie would extend God's blessing in return.

> I don't take too much time, I would just say hi . . . You know, you make life happy yourself and make it happy to [other] people. That's what Hank did. He would take my hand in his and say, Gracie, I love you, and I would say Hank, I love you too. He know my face right away. He said Gracie, he never see a woman working so hard for her kids. Lot of people don't believe in giving love to other people. But that's the way Hank was. . .
>
> He was a beautiful man. He didn't want nobody to know he helped. He quiet about that. People compare his daughters with him. You can't compare like that. I love him, I love his daughters, I love Hank's kids, but not like I loved Hank because Hank is very special. Hank helped a lot of people. A lot of my people. Hank helped a lot of Mexican people, and he was quiet about his giving . . .

When the union tried [to organize], you know, I talked to people about the union and how we didn't need it. Hank didn't want it. And I had some people turn against me because I said we didn't need a union. I said it because my heart told me we didn't need a union. I follow my heart.

I remember when I have my operation, I see the face of my son, of my daughter, and in front of me, right there in front of me, was Hank's face . . . Like family, you know. And I told my son, I only see three faces. My son, my daughter and Hank. Nobody else.

The unions of which Gracie spoke have made several unsuccessful attempts to organize Mexican Industries—most recently in 1995. A month before the employees voted on the question, California-based journalist Raoul Lowery Contreras wrote a vivid essay for *El Central*, Detroit's premier Hispanic newspaper, accurately prophesying why that 1995 vote, too, would fail:

When I was a little boy, I used to catch the streetcar in front of my house and head for the ballpark to see my San Diego Padres play. They were a farm club of the Cleveland Indians then, and they brought into baseball dozens of young players who would make their mark in baseball. Ted Williams was one of them. Hank Aguirre was another.

I wanted to be like my man Hank when I grew up, knowing that he came from the streets like I did and played on dirt lots like I did. He had a good career, ending with the Chicago Cubs. I'll never forget him. After he retired, I lost track of him and did not know that he settled in Detroit. Nor did I know that he started a little business. Nor did I know that his company grew into a giant enterprise of 1,500 employees—most of whom were Hispanic.

When I found out, I was amazed. But I was not amazed to hear from Hispanic Detroiters that Hank Aguirre was one heck of a *patron*—boss, if you will. He took good care of his workers. He took care of his people. So well, in fact, that three times a union tried to organize his workers and three times the union lost. Now, in the wake of his death [in 1994], the union has descended on the company like a vulture to pick the company's bones clean.

I have some general observations about the American labor movement that may interest my friends and readers in Detroit, for there, there is a struggle for the soul of a company founded and run by a *paisano* of whom I was very proud. I speak, of course, of the late Hank Aguirre.

Hank Aguirre was his own best union, and that's why the union organizers never succeeded while he was alive. It would be a shame if they won now. The Aguirre family hasn't changed since he died, has it? The management philosophy hasn't changed since he died, has it?

I don't know his daughters, Pam and Robin and Jill, or his son, Rance, but I do remember a skinny young baseball player named Aguirre who autographed my baseball in the San Diego Padres ballpark and who told some security guy I was his cousin so I could go out on the field before a game and shag balls for him. I do remember that.

Another of Hank's "ladies" was Martha Silva. Born in Guadalajara, Martha migrated to California and moved from there to Detroit. Through a friend, both Martha and her husband landed jobs at Mexican Industries. Martha's husband would leave the company for another job, but Martha stayed on and eventually became a supervisor. (At this writing, she supervises nearly a hundred of her fellow employees.)

Although she had heard a great deal about him, she didn't meet Hank until she was transferred to the Howard plant. He spent considerable time on the plant floor, talking to employees and keeping his finger on the pulse of the business. Some accused him of being obsessed with neatness because of his insistence on plant cleanliness, inside and out. But according to Martha, nothing was considered without taking the well-being of the employees into account first.

I can vouch for this from one of the many telephone calls Hank made to me. We were discussing some new business that had come into the shop, but which Hank wasn't too keen on:

All of them [the sales people], they just want more business and more business and more business. I told them the other day, "Don't quote no more business". . . . They think I'm nuts, and I say to them, Maybe I am nuts, but we can't handle what we've got.

. . . They sold a ten-million-dollar job to Lear. Then I asked those guys, Where are you putting this business? It wasn't until after the sale that they started taking a long look at how many lines and how many machines and how many people. Eighty-six people. Where are we going to put them? How are we going to feed them? Where are they going to park? What bathrooms are they going to use? If they don't have cars, what about bus lines or sharing rides? They gotta get here and I want to make sure the working situation is okay when they do.

Martha spoke to me of how Hank visited with employees on the plant floor, asking about them and their families. Although he wasn't so open to everyone, many times he'd draw up a chair beside Martha, and while she did her sewing he would talk about his roots. He confided his concerns about his own children. He shared both the good and the bad. He talked about La Chona, an area of Encarnacion de Diaz where he had spent some time with his father during his summers as a child. He recalled the dirt streets and the heat and the unsanitary conditions. He had never looked on those early days of his youth in Mexico as an unconquerable hardship, he said; that was what life had offered as a starting point, and he had learned to handle the mix of hope and disappointment as he struggled to improve his condition.

Aguirre Plaza, as attractive as it is, is not truly the best memorial of Hank's presence. Such stories as he told Martha Silva and others—stories of struggle and worry, but also of hope for a better future—were the cave drawings that Hank Aguirre left behind him.

Chapter Ten
The Ominous Rumble of Earthquakes

By 1986, Mexican Industries had acquired a second plant, one in Dearborn, Michigan. It was on Rotunda Drive, in sight of the original Ford Motor Company headquarters. The plant began by producing die-cut insulation, then floor mats, and still later carpeting and tire covers. The carpeting has since been phased out, but the other products are still being produced.

Hank was named 1987's "Hispanic Businessman of the Year" by the U. S. Hispanic Chamber of Commerce. The criteria for the award included both providing leadership and success in developing business in the Hispanic business sector. Those endorsing his candidacy included James Blanchard, governor of Michigan; Lee Iacocca, president of Chrysler; and Coleman Young, mayor of Detroit.

Hank was scheduled to receive the award at the group's eighth annual convention in early October in Los Angeles. At about 7 AM on October 2, the day the awards were to be presented at an evening banquet, an earthquake registering 6.5 on the Richter scale hit Los Angeles, and all guests were ordered to vacate the Bonaventure Hotel, where Hank, members of his family, and others in his party had rooms.

Hank, his daughter Pamela, and her month-old son Brett had rooms on the twenty-seventh floor. No one was permitted to use the elevators, so Hank grabbed Brett, and he and Pam raced on foot down twenty-six flights of stairs, leaving their belongings behind. When they reached ground level, they saw a huge chandelier that had graced the lobby now lying, smashed into pieces, on the floor. No guests were permitted back into the hotel following the earthquake, and so while Hank received the award, the ceremony never took place. A few days later, Hank's son Rance was allowed to enter the damaged hotel and retrieve his father's award, a silver bust of a mythical Aztec warrior chief. Today the bust rests on a pedestal in the Aguirre Plaza lobby.

In January of 1988, a third Mexican Industries plant opened, at the junction of Howard and Rosa Parks Boulevard in Detroit. This plant opened in response to Ford's suggestion that the company get into the leather-wrap steering-wheel production. Like the Howard plant, this plant is located in sight of the Ambassador Bridge. A former warehouse, it is clean, bright, and air-conditioned.

Hank had, characteristically, been somewhat hesitant about this venture, thinking it too labor-intensive. The business started slowly, and Hank wasn't too keen on the low volume. He liked it still less when Ford decided to give another supplier the Lincoln and Continental wheels, leaving Mexican Industries an exclusive on the Bronco II wheel. Luck smiled again, however: The Bronco II would become the Explorer, one of the most successful vehicles ever made and a enormous source of business for Mexican Industries.

In June of 1988, a fourth plant was opened, this one on the east side of Dearborn. Products such as carpeted spare-tire covers, sound-deadener items, and insulation were produced out of this, the Stecker plant. The company was ranked 68 among the state's 100 fastest-growing young companies by *Michigan Business* magazine. In October of 1988, the Small Business Administration named Hank its "Michigan Minority Small Business Person of the Year." That same year, he was honored by the National Minority Business Council.

More awards came: The National Minority Supplier Development Council (NMSDC) Award for business leadership. The Alliance of Commercial Hispanic Americans Award. The International Heritage Hall of Fame Award. And many others. There were countless honorary resolutions and testimonials, and invitations for speaking engagements arrived in the mail almost daily.

All this outward success had its price. As Hank became more and more intensely involved in his company and in uncounted civic and humanitarian efforts, his marriage was shaking into pieces. Legal papers for divorce were filed in the winter of 1986, although the divorce did not become final until the summer of 1989.

Both Hank and Barbara attended many sessions in a marriage counselor's chambers, but, despite the bond of their children, they had grown too far apart, and in too many ways. Hank was a benevolent controller, but a controller nonetheless. He clung to the old-fashioned traditions of marriage, in which a wife's duty is taking care of home and family, while Barbara needed to feel free of the trappings of a housewife. So Barbara was criticized for her lack of interest in cooking, sewing, cleaning, and other domestic tasks. She performed these chores, but she didn't like it. Hank and I occasionally talked after one of his reconciliation trips to Scottsdale, Arizona (where they had another home, to which she moved during their separation). He would speak to me of his frustration.

On the other hand, the day-to-day raising of the Aguirre children had also been Barbara's responsibility, and she had handled that situation very well. Each of the children had his or her own problems growing up—some quite serious—and Barbara dealt with them as well as any concerned mother could have.

When it became evident that the marriage wasn't going to survive, Hank moved out of the family house in Franklin and bought another house a few miles away.

The rapid growth of Mexican Industries forced Hank to realize he couldn't handle it all alone. He needed an extraordinarily capable person to help him handle the day-to-day operations of the company. He began a quiet search for that person early in 1989, interviewing several candidates, but the right one didn't come along until the fall of 1990.

The man who was to succeed Hank hadn't even heard of Mexican Industries until shortly before he was hand-picked by Hank. He was running a company called Power Lawnmower, Inc.—a lawnmower replacement parts business, in Rochester, New York. The business was up for sale, and when the sale took place, he was out of a job. He'd done essentially the same job earlier for another company in transition: keeping the business running until it was sold. One of the investors in that company, Wes Van Houtin, lived in Detroit. When Van Houtin ran into Bob Hagedorn, a certified public accountant for Hank, the two had lunch together. Bob mentioned Hank's search for a general manager and Van Houtin made a recommendation.

James A. Merkhofer was living in Birmingham, Alabama, and running a business in Rochester, New York, when he received a phone call from Detroit. Hank conducted the interview himself, and he also had references for him from a mutual business acquaintance. So with only one interview, Hank had heard enough, and hired Jim Merkhofer as the first general manager ever, and Hank's second-in-command, at Mexican Industries.

Along with this good business news, however, there were ominous rumblings in Detroit that disturbed Hank deeply. Rumors began to buzz that Tom Monaghan, the owner of the

Detroit Tigers, had plans to relocate Hank's old team to another city.

In response, Hank called a press conference on the morning of December 27, 1990, announcing that he would make a bid to buy the ball club. In a televised news report later that day, Mort Crim of WDTV-Detroit quizzed Hank about his announcement, and he explained that his move had been spurred by the firing of Ernie Harwell, the popular radio announcer for the Tigers, and by the possibility that the Tigers might move elsewhere.

Hank wanted, he told the TV anchorman, a renewal in Detroit—not an exodus from it. He noted that Hudson's (a popular department store) had left, Sears had left, and Cadillac was about to leave the city. The Detroit Lions, the city's football team, had left. So had the Detroit Pistons basketball team. Hank believed that the Detroit Tigers belonged to Detroit: Owners might come and go, but the city gave the team its ground, its heritage, its roots. He condemned even the casual notion that the team might leave. Hank also said he had called Mayor Coleman Young to tell him of his intentions, and that Young had expressed his support.

The former mayor told me, in an interview, of his years of acquaintance with Hank—both as ballplayer and as businessman. Mayor Young suggested that Hank Aguirre's business acumen ultimately contributed much more to his fellow man than did his sports celebrity. "He understood the needs of this town," Young said. He added that perhaps Hank, as a pro athlete in a sports-minded city, understood what it meant to feel—and to need—community support, and that Hank had honorably returned that support. Hank's motivation to succeed was intertwined with his love for the place, Young said; and his sacrifices to assist the community were made without fanfare.

Without discounting his career in baseball, I think his best days were after he left the Tigers. These were the most fruitful for himself and for this community. When you think of what this man accomplished, providing jobs in this city, I would say it was his shining hour . . . What he did after he left the Tigers, so few people are aware of, and ought to be told.

The mayor recalled how Hank had supported a program for establishing recreation centers for disadvantaged youths throughout Detroit, "largely in the low-income sections of the city." Such centers became possible through awards from the national government under President Jimmy Carter. One is the Roberto Clemente Center, located on Bagley Street on Detroit's lower west side, in the heart of "Mexicantown."

Tom Monaghan announced at the time that he had no intention of moving the Tigers. Ultimately, however, he did in fact sell the team to Mike Ilitch—owner of the Red Wings (Detroit's pro hockey team) and of the Little Caesar's pizza franchise—in 1992. When Hank got word of the impending sale, he contacted Ilitch, wanting to invest, but the deal was already done.

In September of 1991, Jim Merkhofer saw the first Mexican Industries plant open out of the state of Michigan. This one was located in Tempe, Arizona. A few miles south of Tempe lies the small town of Guadalupe. When Hank was made aware of the desperate needs of Guadalupe's schools, he donated several thousands of dollars toward its educational fund. (More recently his daughter Robin, now vice-president at Mexican Industries, picked up the tab for a baseball complex for the town's Little League program.)

Sometimes Hank's ability to predict the future was uncanny. In March of 1992, he opened yet another plant—this one in Dearborn—specifically to produce car airbags. Today, the Miller plant accounts for $12 million in annual sales.

During this period, Hank had met and begun seeing a young woman named Tina Bessega, who worked in an office near Mexican Industries' Bagley plant. Tina worked at the headquarters of Chuck Muir, a popular restaurateur who operated numerous locations throughout Michigan. She and Hank met for the first time when both were having lunch in the Hummer sports bar and grill, near the plant.

Hank had deep feelings for his family. He loved both his children and Barbara deeply. With the final judgment of his divorce came remorse, a sense of failure, and self-examination. Torn by these emotions, Hank moved out of the house he had bought, away from Tina, and back into the original family home in Franklin. Ultimately, however, Hank asked Tina to become his wife.

Hank and Tina were married in a civil ceremony at the Ritz-Carlton Hotel in Dearborn on October 24, 1992. It was a huge affair, with many of Hank's old baseball friends in attendance—Ferguson Jenkins, Al Kaline, Bill Freehan, and others. As part of the marriage rite, I was given the honor of reading from Paul's first letter to the Corinthians:

> Love is always patient and kind. Love is never jealous. Love is never boastful or conceited. It is never selfish. Love does not take offense. It is not resentful. Love takes no pleasure in another person's pain, but delights in the truth. Love is always ready to excuse, to trust, to hope, and to endure whatever comes. Love has no end.

Their marriage was blessed by a priest at Mass the next morning in the couple's parish church.

Chapter Eleven
A Sincere Man

The zest and love that Hank displayed for Tina, after his long and troubled period of soul-searching, showed up in the rest of his life as well. Hank was a true romantic in his outlook. He and I often traveled together by jet on business trips, and one of his favorite activities on such flights was to put on a headset and find a Latin music channel. Hank loved all Latin music. (One good friend of his was the singer Trini Lopez, known for such popular Latin-flavored songs as "Lemon Tree" and "If I Had a Hammer.") Soon after takeoff, his entire body would be moving to the beat. Shortly thereafter, he would begin directing an imaginary orchestra with great sweeps of his arms. With enough stimulus, he might even burst into song, strong and off-key. His good humor, however, seemed to keep fellow passengers from ever becoming annoyed.

One of his longtime favorite songs, which he always sang with great gusto, was "Guantanamera," an international hit in the late 1960s by Jose Fernandez Diaz, Julian Orbon, and Pete Seeger, based on a lyric by the great Cuban poet Jose Martí:

> Yo soy un hombre sincero
> De donde crecen las palmas
> Y antes de morirme quiero
> Echar mis versos del alma

> I am a sincere man
> From where the palm trees grow
> And before I die I want
> To pour out these verses from my soul . . .

He was fascinated by faraway places and their romantic names. We'd be on a flight, and suddenly out of nowhere would come: "What about the South China Sea, Bob?"

"What about it?"

"It sounds like a place I'd like to be. Like: 'Where've you been, Hank?' 'Oh, I've been sailing the South China Sea.' See what I mean? Doesn't that sound *great?* Or maybe the Serengeti, or Kilimanjaro . . . or The Dry Tortugas. You know that *tortuga* means *turtle* in Spanish, don't you, Bob?"

"Nope, I didn't know that, Hank."

"Wouldn't it be something if a tortuga was a turtle in Turkey, too? Or in Tutuila?"

"Um, alliterative, you mean."

"How about Mandalay? It must be a special place. Kipling wrote a poem about the road that went there. To Mandalay. Maybe I'll go there someday."

I think that, as much as the places themselves, it was the wordplay and the sound of those strange names that held an allure for Hank. And like anyone who enjoyed wordplay, Hank also understood the value of plain speaking. When Kaizen—a manufacturing method introduced by the Japanese—became a fad among business leaders, Hank was called upon to speak to a group of suppliers about this exotic "new method" Mexican Industries had adopted. He spoke in such concrete terms that his message was unmistakably clear. And to illustrate how to not to get lost in meaningless business jargon, he used the analogy of "Flimflam vs. Plain English." He employed a chart illustrating how to translate misleading double-talk:

Flimflam	Plain English
Net-Profit Revenue Deficiencies	We're losing money.
Negative Patient-Care Outcome	He's dead.
Statistical Misrepresentation	It's a lie.
Strategic Hypothesis	I'm guessing.
Abrupt Malfunction Syndrome	It stopped working.

Hank's point was that that it's easy to get caught up in rhetoric and vague theory. He added: "Continue to produce products of quality, and growth will follow."

However much the road to Mandalay might have called to him, Hank was dedicated to his country as he was to the growth of Mexican Industries. Speaking at a national convention of the National Minority Supplier Development Council (NMSDC) in Orlando, Hank spoke plainly and from the heart on "Buying American":

> We Americans get turned on with slam dunks, Hail-Mary passes, and home runs. And there's nothing wrong with that—except they don't win games over the long haul. Make no mistake about it, we minorities are in this for the long haul—or ought to be, because history shows we've had to struggle for every inch of progress, and we've walked many lonely miles to get where we are today . . .
>
> I look at [the NMSDC] partnership not in the sense that we should use it militantly; or to get handouts from corporate America's boardrooms. I look at that power as fuel that drives our engines of progress. And progress is measured by the yardstick of quality. We either deliver quality or we die.
>
> I see it as a power that generates skills, that makes us more technically based, more determined to continue to improve upon what we do. We're aware of the continuous-improvement hammer that's suspended over our heads. And last, and perhaps most important, is the enormous power of our purchasing dollars that are generated through us minority suppliers. That's what I'm going to talk about here and now: our purchasing power, as it relates to building a stronger America.
>
> You will be surprised to discover how we are using this huge reservoir of purchasing dollars to cripple ourselves. To defeat ourselves. To endanger our very livelihoods. I'm talking about our track record when it comes to buying home-grown products. Of buying American! . . .
>
> Let me put this in terms of how we hurt ourselves when we don't buy American—and remember, I'm talking about

only one product here. Starting with the actual assembly of [an automobile], we lose about two weeks' work per car per worker. Which means those imports we buy add up to a direct loss of about eleven-thousand jobs. But that's just the beginning.

When you add to that number the parts suppliers, the plastic-manufacturers, the leather-tanners, the steelmakers, the weavers and spinners of cloths, the engineers, the tire-makers—when we count this domino effect of lost jobs, we begin to understand the enormity of the ripple effect that becomes a tidal wave of self-defeat, because the damage continues to radiate outward. What about those businesses that are tied to the workers who are idled?

I'm talking about the store that sells the pop, the retailers who sell the clothing and the furniture, the grocers who sell the meat, the soap and the bread. The shoemaker who repairs the shoes. All of these and others like them feel the squeeze, and they've got to let people go. . .

Can you see what we are doing to ourselves? Can you see the need to carry the "Buy American" torch throughout our companies? Together we have the power to light the fire of economic strength for hundreds of thousands of American minorities who are losing their jobs to overseas manufacturers because of some misguided sense of saving a buck. Let's use our minority buying power to benefit all of us—including the majority!

In speaking plainly, though—especially to his fellow workers—Hank tried whenever possible to make his points positively. Sometimes *plain speaking* is simply a euphemism for boorishness rather than sincerity. I recall one meeting that Hank and I, as clients, attended at Ford Motor Company headquarters in Dearborn. For managers from across the United States were in attendance at this important annual event. Lee Iacocca, who then headed the Ford Division, came onstage immediately after another speaker, John McLean, had congratulated his colleagues on their hard work over the past year.

Iacocca strode to the podium and looked at the word CON-GRATULATIONS projected on a large screen behind him. His opening shot was: "I don't know how much that lousy 'con-gratulations' slide cost, but if it was more than a lousy half-a-buck, it was too much, because you guys don't deserve to be congratulated." The remainder of Iacocca's remarks (which were rather salty, to put it mildly) went downhill from there.

Afterwards, Hank was in shock from Iacocca's display. He couldn't believe what he had heard. "How did that guy get where he is? He knows one word: *lousy*. Lousy market. Lousy competition. Lousy sales. Lousy product. Those lousy !@#$%#! Even if something was good, it was *lousy!*"

Hank's encouraging, common-sense gospel of hard work for mutual benefit seemed to be working magnificently for his own company. In May of 1993, yet another Mexican Industries plant opened—this one in Melvindale, Michigan, a few miles south of Detroit. That same month, Hank checked in at Henry Ford Hospital for his routine annual physical, and it was apparently without incident. It was Hank's habit to take an annual physical every May, without exception.

Hank's longtime physician had routinely ordered a PSA test for Hank in the past. (PSA stands for Prostate-Specific Antigen, a blood test used as an early cancer-detection method.) However, that doctor underwent heart surgery, and because his own health problems, he had stopped serving as Hank's regular physician. Hank began seeing other doctors instead, and his medical records show that, with the switchover in doctors, the last PSA test he had taken was in 1990.

A month after his uneventful May 1993 physical, Hank began to complain about a pain in his back. He went back to Henry Ford Hospital soon thereafter, and a series of tests indicated a problem. A biopsy was conducted, and a malignancy was detected. The diagnosis was cancer of the prostate. A subsequent bone scan (employing radioactive material injected into the blood stream) at the hospital seemed to indicate that the cancer had not spread.

As Tina and Hank left the hospital, waiting at the entrance for their car, they both wept with relief, rejoicing in the apparent good news. The rejoicing would be short-lived.

Chapter Twelve
Flight 37

Seeking a second opinion, Hank and Tina traveled to Northwestern University in Chicago a few weeks later, in July of 1993. There they met with Dr. John Marquardt, who had been affiliated with the Chicago Cubs, where Hank had spent some of his major league career. Hank and Tina carried with them the same bone scan that was taken at Henry Ford Hospital.

That bone scan, according to Dr. Marquardt, indicated that Hank had metastatic prostate cancer—*metastatic* meaning the disease had already invaded Hank's bones. Hank and Tina then went to the Mayo Clinic in Rochester, Minnesota. Dr. Marquardt's diagnosis was confirmed, and radiation was recommended.

News of Hank's illness swept through the world of professional baseball and was picked up by the wire services and broadcast coast to coast. The news heightened national awareness of prostate cancer. Get-well cards arrived by the hundreds. National political figures—including Michigan governor John Engler, U. S. Secretary of Commerce Ron Brown, and Congressman John Dingell—wrote and called. Harriet Michel, president of the National Minority Supplier Development Council, wrote. A card came from Mark "The Bird" Fidrich, another beloved onetime starting pitcher for the Tigers. Ted Williams called. Officials and former teammates of the Chicago Cubs and Detroit Tigers wrote to encourage Hank.

121

Perhaps even more touching were the letters Hank received from children, some of them recipients of scholarships Hank had provided at the Holy Redeemer School in Detroit's "Mexicantown." A young man named Harrison Schneider wrote:

> Dear Hank,
>   Thank you for the baseball and stuff. You are a kind man for giving me a singhd [sic] ball. Thanks for giving me your address. I herd [sic] you are very sick and I give you hope because you were a great baseball player.

At Mexican Industries, employees showered him with religious artifacts blessed by the clergy, and his "ladies" prepared special foods for him. Supposed miracle cures by the hundreds were sent in from all over the United States. Countless friends sent word to him of their requests for special Masses to be said for his recovery. One woman, Sheila Dovey, wrote:

> Some people wonder if one person can really make a difference in the world, but I think it's possible because I've seen the difference you make in the lives of those around you. You don't just talk about making the world a better place, you do something about it by reaching out and giving of yourself. Hank, I just wanted you to know you are a very special person and a real inspiration to me. I feel blessed that God allowed you to touch a part of my life.

The city hoped. All over the country, friends and fans hoped. But Hank grew weaker and thinner, losing his hair from the chemotherapy and radiation, and all the while still trying to run Mexican Industries from his home or his hospital bed.

In addition to his own health, Hank had to be concerned about the health of his creation, Mexican Industries, and all the employees and others who depended on him. To allay widespread worries and rumors about his company, Hank directed

me to write a letter that was sent to all of Mexican Industries'
clients in January of 1994. It read in part:

> The reports in the press and on local TV about my bout
> with cancer are accurate. On the other hand, I am respond-
> ing very positively to the prescribed treatment. Consequently,
> I plan to be very active in the day-to-day operations at
> Mexican Industries for some time to come. I'm writing to
> assure you of that.
>
> However, in the event that something unforeseen would
> incapacitate me, an already existing succession plan will kick
> in to provide uninterrupted service. This plan includes a team
> that is already in place and that is capable, polished, sea-
> soned and, to a healthy extent, redundant in the critical
> areas of administration, engineering, manufacturing,
> research, and development and production.

In June, Hank would formally name Jim Merkhofer as his
successor to the presidency of Mexican Industries, putting to
rest concerns about the company's long-term plans. (In his role
as general manager, Jim Merkhofer participated in the firm's
growth in sales from $38 million in 1990 to $150 million in
1995.) Even after choosing his successor, however, Hank continued to be active.

Hank's patron saint was Our Lady of Guadalupe. Her stat-
ue or likeness can be found in every Mexican Industries
facility. In April of 1994, Hank, with friends and family, made
a pilgrimage to her shrine, near Mexico City. He undertook this
journey in search of a cure. Surely the pilgrimage at least
graced him with spiritual strength, for his greatest struggles
with illness still lay ahead.

Hank's battle with cancer was monumental. The details of
his ordeal may serve as a terrible reminder to readers of how
insidious this disease can be, and how brave Hank was in facing it. In particular, I interviewed three people who had
first-hand knowledge of Hank's struggle. One was Jeanne

Parzuchowski, cancer coordinator at Harper Hospital. Another was Diane Finkel, a registered nurse and Hank's private caregiver during his last days. The third was Dr. Bruce Redman, the cancer specialist who was Hank's physician to the end.

Hank and Tina came to meet Jeanne Parzuchowski through her husband, Jim, who worked at Ford. When Jim learned of Hank's illness during a conversation with Jay Bocci, Jim gave him his wife's business card, explaining that Jeanne worked at one of the top cancer centers in the country—Harper Hospital, right in Hank's hometown of Detroit.

The day Hank came into Harper's oncology clinic, he saw Dr. Bruce Redman, an oncologist on staff at the hospital, and Jeanne Parzuchowski as well. Jeanne remember that some of the nurses were quite impressed at seeing *the* Hank Aguirre, a genuine baseball star, in their unit. Hank graciously autographed menus, baseballs, photographs, letters from kids, even the top of a nurse's scrub suit. When visitors to other patients learned that Hank Aguirre was on the same floor and asked for his autograph, Hank accommodated them all, as long as he was able.

Bruce Redman—a tall, raw-boned man with a heavy mustache—first examined Hank on April 29, 1994. Hank had already been diagnosed as having metastatic prostate cancer. At the time he came into the hospital, Hank was placed on androgen-deprivation therapy and had an initially positive response. Unfortunately, patients become resistant, or "refractory," to such therapy. (The median survival rate for men afflicted with incurable hormone-refractory prostate cancer is about fifty percent beyond six to eight months—fifty percent will die in six months, and the remaining fifty percent within a year.) Hank then agreed to participate in trial drug therapy, and had a positive response. Unfortunately, however, the response was only brief.

With such patients, Dr. Redman deals in today. If there's pain, he seeks to relieve it. If another symptom arises, he concentrates on what can be done to make that symptom go away today. Whether medication is applied to relieve the pain or to shrink the cancer, the goal is always the same: to improve the *quality* of life, because no one has control of the *quantity* of life remaining.

And so at Harper Hospital, Hank was helped mostly to control his pain, so he could do what he wanted to do. He directed Dr. Redman to keep him as free of symptoms as possible, so that he could keep functioning and contributing. During his visits to the clinic, Dr. Redman recalled, Hank would talk to other patients, building their hope and morale, even while he was in great pain and speaking from a wheelchair. Hank continued to involve himself in community work, and to call the shots at Mexican Industries, right up to the last.

Tim Seagraves, a friend of Rance Aguirre, recalled one memorable hospital visit. While Tim and Rance were visiting, a young orderly dropped in to ask Hank for his autograph. After signing, Hank asked the orderly to name his favorite all-time Detroit Tiger.

He didn't hesitate: "Al Kaline," he said.

"Would you like to meet him someday?" Hank asked with his characteristic grin.

"Oh, boy, Mr. Aguirre, would I ever! Can you arrange it for me?"

Hank pointed to a man sitting in a chair by the window: Fellow Tiger Al Kaline just happened to be visiting Hank at the time.

"Meet your favorite Tiger, Al Kaline," Hank said.

Al rose and shook the kid's hand, and the orderly was speechless. Hank's chuckle was the only sound in the room as the orderly walked away, shaking his head in awe.

Hank's spirit was also evident one day when Gracie Zuniga visited him in the hospital, bringing with her some Mexican food. Because of his heavy medication and radiation, Hank's appetite hardly existed. He had lost considerable weight and had been refusing meals from the best sources. But when one of his "ladies" brought food prepared in her own kitchen, Hank ate a substantial amount with gusto. He ate because he knew Gracie had taken the time to prepare it. He ate it so she would not be disappointed. Gracie recalls:

> Tina was there and his son was there. And Hank asked me how work was going at [the] Howard [plant] . . . He was talking in Spanish, you know. He worried about Howard. He worried about all his plants. Not how the plants were doing, but how the people were doing.

From time to time Hank displayed a short temper, but who wouldn't? He was scarcely eating or sleeping, and pain was his constant companion; but he never complained. He tried to make things better for others. His strength in the face of what confronted him was unreal. It was during these final months, more than ever, that he truly earned the laudatory nickname given to him during his baseball career, "The Tall Mexican."

By late July of 1994, Hank had only two desires: He hoped to attend the dedication of Mexican Industries' new corporate headquarters, so long in the planning, and he wished to spend the rest of his remaining time at home. Both desires were fulfilled. With the exception of two emergency visits to the hospital, he was able to stay at his home.

In the early evening of August 3, 1994, Mexican Industries' new corporate headquarters was to be dedicated. Almost ten months had passed since Hank and Dennis Archer (Detroit's future mayor) had broken ground at the corner of Rosa Parks and Howard with a stainless-steel shovel.

Hank was determined to make the dedication. His legs and feet had swollen to twice their normal size from hydration and as a result of his being bedridden. Yet he refused to be wheeled into his building, nor would he wear slippers when he walked from the van into the foyer.

The responsibility for seeing that these things happened fell on the shoulders of Diane Finkel, who had been assigned that very day to be Hank's private nurse. Diane was assigned to buy shoes big enough to fit Hank's swollen feet. Bob Lanier, star player for the Detroit Pistons basketball team, could have slipped his feet into those size-22 shoes with ease. But they weren't slippers, and that was important to Hank. Jeanne Parzuchowski also accompanied Hank to the opening. "I chose a pink silk dress because it was a bright color," she told me, "and Diane had selected a dressy outfit, because the two of us were going to attend incognito. Like nobody would know who we were or what our function was [as Hank's caregivers]. And it worked."

When the van pulled up to the front entrance of the building, Hank got out with the aid of a walker, and, flanked by Jeanne and Diane, entered the new corporate headquarters of Mexican Industries, standing tall. The packed foyer resounded with applause.

That was a hard day for Hank. He was speaking about a future he knew he wouldn't share. Many forces pressed on him. His pain intensified, he grew nauseous, and he was emotionally torn. He paid for that day in many ways. Yet, he persevered. He was cordial to a host of well-wishers. He didn't turn aside the many people who wanted to have their picture taken with him. He signed some autographs.

The new mayor of Detroit, Dennis Archer, was there with his wife for the dedication. Mayor Archer spoke of all that Mexican Industries had done to revive Detroit, employing hundreds and renewing a neighborhood given up for dead by many. Sports celebrities and business leaders participated in the ceremonies. Father Bob Halter of Holy Redeemer blessed the new facility. As Mexican Industries' second-in-command, Jim

Merkhofer also welcomed visitors. It was a signal event for the city of Detroit, but the miracle unrecognized by most was simply that Hank made it to the ceremonies. There was no doubt in Tina's mind, though, that he would be there. Hank was running the show, and whatever he wanted got top priority.

Hank's episodes with pain were monumental, and Dr. Bruce Redman helped him to manage the pain as it progressed. At first, pain-control was achieved through oral medication. As the disease progressed and the pain became more intense, he was fitted with an epidural catheter, to introduce pain-killing medication directly around the nerve roots of the spinal column. This allowed Hank to function with alertness and comprehension. Hank had the procedure done on Thursday, August 11. When he was discharged from the hospital, Hank's pain was under control.

One morning as we sat in the kitchen of his Bloomfield Hills home, I asked him to share his thoughts with me as he battled his disease. He was sipping a glass of water, and he placed the glass in front of him.

"Bob, it changes a lot of things," he replied. "What I thought was important is not important."

He sipped again from the glass, and said he recognized that he had been blessed in many ways. He spoke of his "God-given" ability to pitch, and of what that gift had brought to him. He spoke of those who had been willing to reach out to help him so he could help others. He spoke of time and how precious it was.

Then he pointed to the glass of water. It was about a third full, and he compared it to an hourglass through which sand was pouring. Hank expressed his hope that he'd get done what he wanted to do before all the sand lay at the bottom of that hourglass. His dark brown eyes welled up with tears as he spoke.

He cleared his throat and wiped his eyes and spoke of Jim Merkhofer and the faith he placed in him. He talked of all his children, and of the guilt he carried for "botching it as a father." He said that he considered himself responsible for their misfortunes because he had away so much during their early years. He talked of the long walks he took with Rance in an attempt to counsel and support his son, who had a drug addiction.

Hank and I had talked many times about the problem. I was involved in a twelve-step program made up primarily of parents with drug-addicted children. At Hank and Pam's request, I had twice set up interventions for the family to do some soul-searching confrontations with Rance. I tried to explain that I believed it was imperative to let go—to allow his son to be responsible for his own actions and choices, good or bad. (Ultimately, Rance checked into a recovery center in Arizona, and he came out several weeks later clean and in recovery.)

Hank turned and looked out the kitchen window. He drained the glass of water, set the empty glass in front of him, and studied it for a long time.

As a result of his cancer, Hank's bones lost most of their density. The depletion of calcium from the bone is called *hypercalcemia*, and its loss means that a bone simply cannot carry weight. Hank's bones became like honeycombed straws. In his final weeks, Hank endured several agonizing bone fractures attributable to the disease. Many may have occurred, not even from Hank's movements, but simply from the weight of his own body bearing down upon his bones as he lay in bed. That's how fragile he became.

Hypercalcemia is considered a true cancer emergency, one that is treated with the same urgency as, say, an airway blockage. Aside from what it does to bone, hypercalcemia also affects all the body's smooth muscles: the heart, the bowel, the bladder. It affects the thought processes, causing sleepiness, lethargy, and confusion, and bringing generalized weakness. Hank was at home when the effects of this cancer-related malady hit him. It was hypercalcemia-related episodes that compelled Tina and Diane to take Hank to the hospital for his last emergency visits.

Hank's caregivers were dedicated to making whatever time was left as comfortable as their skills would permit. The epidural catheter, with its direct pain-killing medication, provided Hank with enough awareness and focus to take care of what he could, to come to terms with what he couldn't, and to accept the realization of his cancer's ultimate course. Hank's thoughts were not of death, however, but of living.

Diane spoke to me, for example, of a retirement party held for Ben Gonzalez, a close friend of Hank and an employee of Mexican Industries. Hank Aguirre had never been one to miss a good party, and he was determined that he wasn't going to miss Ben's:

> Before we went to the party, we stopped at Mexican Industries. We went into the plant and Hank was surrounded by the people. I remember him picking out something that was wrong. Some little thing, like he just had to do that. I remember us walking through the plant and into the foyer. He proceeded slowly looking at the pictures on the walls, peering in the offices, making his way back to the office he would never occupy—his office. He paused at the door and inspected what lay inside. It was furnished in beautiful cherry: the desk, the credenza, the round conference table. He entered and he circled slowly around that table, touching it. It was almost a caress. He was laboring now, and yet he never sat down. He moved to his desk and walked behind it and held the back of the chair for support. His chair. You knew he would never sit in that chair to conduct business. He knew, too. Yet he was smiling.

There were several friends and family members in the office, and Hank finally agreed to some picture-taking. Someone shoved his desk chair around to the side, and he finally sat down. Of the countless pictures taken of Hank that evening, not one showed anything but a smile.

On Monday morning, August 29, 1994, Hank's condition worsened, and Diane called Dr. Redman. Hank had some unspoken but vital business to take care of, she sensed, and he was holding off. Diane also urged the doctor to talk to Tina, who was suffering under the enormous strain of her husband's illness. Tina didn't want to broach the subject of Hank's "undone business" either, because it carried with it the shadow of closure. The doctor told Diane to bring Hank in to the hospital. Hank went into Dr. Redmond's office alone first. About twenty minutes passed. Hank came out of the office and Tina went in. He was as supportive as he could be under the circumstances, but what Bruce Redmond had to say to Tina Aguirre was simply to tell her that her husband was dying, and he was going to die soon.

Members of Hank's family began to arrive from California. As they came into his home, Hank seemed to gather strength. "It was incredible," Diane remarked. He got out of bed, got dressed, and walked from the back bedroom out to the living room. He might as well have walked a hundred miles barefoot over razor blades. He sat with his sisters and brothers, and he kidded and laughed with everybody. He cracked jokes and recalled childhood memories. Richard recalled during that last visit that Hank asked him to sit next to him on the bed. Richard put his arms around him and the two of them just sat there.

"I just idolized him," Richard told me, remembering the strong force Hank had been in his life and in the lives of others. "He was more than a brother, He was bigger than that. I remembered the good times and Hank's generosity and concern."

Hank began to talk about his father. He kept wanting to get dressed. "I've got to get dressed. I need my suit," he said. He talked about flying to California. "See if the flight's ready. It's Flight 37." Thirty-seven was his number when he played for the Detroit Tigers. He spoke of an uncle, and two or three others, who lived in California. A brother. A sister. "Tell them I'm coming," he said. "I'm ready. I have to get dressed. I'm ready." He talked about his childhood. He talked about his kids, recalling times when they were small. He talked about Barbara. He rambled about the business and the people who worked there.

Early in the afternoon of Sunday, September 4, Hank kept reaching up. Reaching for something. Either Tina or Diane decided to give Hank something to hold. Neither one knew where it had come from, but there was a red, white, and blue baseball lying on the bed beside him. Tina placed the ball in Hank's hand and closed his fingers around it.

That evening, from about seven o'clock on, he grew very quiet. His breathing changed. Although scheduled to leave the Aguirre home, Diane felt uneasy about going. She told Tina she was too tired to drive home and would stay the night instead.

It was about one o'clock in the morning. Tina, Diane, and Kathy—Hank's night nurse—sat in the bedroom, each woman lost in her own thoughts. The muted television cast the only light in the room. Hank clutched the baseball in his left hand. His eyes were closed. The three women became aware that the TV set was on. When they looked up, they saw that the program in progress was one about baseball. Tina remembers it being *The Lou Gehrig Story*. Diane recalled it had to do with *Great Moments in Baseball*. Whatever it was, an ethereal silence embraced the room. For Hank, that embrace would prevail for all eternity.

Chapter Thirteen
No Continuing City

At about 4 AM, the phone rang at my home. It was Bill Flynn. Very gently, Bill said, "He's gone, Bob." I began by notifying the metro Detroit papers and their suburban counterparts. Then the papers in other cities where Hank had played ball: Chicago, Los Angeles, Phoenix, Reading, and Cleveland. The wire services. Network television and the local affiliates. By noon, Hank's death was being reported throughout the country.

George Ramos of the *Los Angeles Times* wrote a particularly poignant article, headlined "Hank Aguirre: An Even Bigger Hero Off the Diamond." As it happened, 1994 was the year of the great major-league baseball strike, and his piece was typical of the many written about Hank at that time.

> Despite all the bums in baseball—the players who went on strike and the owners who canceled the World Series—there are really some heroes of the game.
>
> Hank Aguirre was one of them.
>
> He's remembered as a lanky southpaw with a blazing fastball. He was selected to the All-Star team while with the Detroit Tigers, where he spent ten of his sixteen years in big-league baseball. But for this ballplayer, who was born into a Mexican immigrant family and reared in San Gabriel, his greatest fame came after his playing days were over . . .
>
> After he quit playing, Aguirre wanted to help Mexican Americans and other minorities. He was grateful for what he had been able to acquire and felt the least he could do was give something back. A distant relative, East L. A. priest

133

Arnold Gonzalez, said Aguirre had a fierce pride in being Mexican, a trait instilled by his father, who was from Jalisco. Father Gonzalez added that Hank wanted others to climb up the ladder of life.

Paul Woody, a sports writer for the *Richmond Times* Dispatch, wrote:

> We live in a time when, too often, the word *substance* is followed by *abuse* when it refers to athletes. And too often we find that some athletes have a depth of character that's about equal to the thickness of their trading cards.
>
> Then there's Aguirre, who favored substance over style and chose to have character instead of being one. If you choose to think of Aguirre as a former baseball player, that's fine. He certainly was that. But if you choose to remember him as a former baseball player whose vision now provides 1,000 people with jobs, retirement funds, and health-care benefits; whose life didn't stop when he quit playing baseball; who could exist and thrive in the real world; and who serves as a better role model than any former star athlete you might see on a home-shopping channel, that might be even better.

There were two funeral masses.

The funeral Mass at Holy Redeemer Church, in southwest Detroit, took place on a bright day with sunshine abounding. People spilled out into the foyer and to the steps outside. Children in uniform from Holy Redeemer school flanked the pallbearers as they moved up the sweeping staircase with Hank's casket. Bells intoned their somber message with a steady, measured dirge. Hank's "ladies," many with scarves over their heads, knelt in prayer. They wept silently, in disbelief that their *patron* was gone. Erik Smith, a veteran reporter for Detroit's ABC affiliate, Channel 7, concluded his coverage by saying: "No, you won't find Hank Aguirre's name in Cooperstown, but in this city, he was a Hall-of-Famer."

Condolences flooded in to Tina, to the Aguirre family, and to Mexican Industries. Among the many special observances of Hank's death, the students of Holy Redeemer High School held a special memorial service, and Carmen Munoz, of Michigan's Commission on Spanish-speaking affairs, started the process to change the name of Howard Street to Aguirre Street.

Aside from these public displays of mourning and commemoration, Hank's nurse Diane Finkel noted privately the stunned reactions of many people close to Hank:

> Neal [MacLean, a young business associate and protégé of Hank] is almost childlike . . . He knows he's losing his mentor, his father figure. Bill [Flynn] is remarkable . . . He gets Tina through each day—someone safe to vent to, and to lay out her feelings of helplessness and hopelessness . . . Jerry [Coyne], Jay [Bocci] and Bill [Freehan] reflect disbelief at what's happened, and great repect. Bob [Copley's] eyes mirror a sadness that makes it difficult for me to make eye contact when the doorbell rings. He loved Hank on a different level . . .

Tina had asked me to be Hank's eulogist. I recall sitting on the front steps of their home, talking it over with her only a few days before Hank died. (Tina has an arresting way of tilting her head down when she begins to speak, and then punctuating the end of her message by raising her head to look straight into your eyes.) I recall sitting in front of the glaring monitor of my computer, my fingers on the keyboard and my mind wafting back through the thirty-two years I had known Hank. My files bulged with letters and speeches. There were requests for donations along with notations of Hank's directives of what amounts to give. Although I could not, for the life of me, think of Hank in the past tense, the memories began to flow.

I'm not going to get maudlin with Hank's eulogy because he would not appreciate that. In fact, on Hank's scale of rating a person's performance, if I were to get maudlin or weepy, I would be classified as a "dunkey."

So instead, I want to talk, foremost, about Hank and about love, because the two are inseparable. I can say this with some degree of certainty because of my knowledge of Hank acquired through our long friendship. *Ay conositos mi amigo Hank por trente dos años . . .*

Hank Aguirre was the most remarkable person I have ever known. I have never had a friend quite like him. His gift of leadership and the manner in which he used that gift went far beyond the extraordinary . . .

His marvelous understanding of the human spirit was evident in countless ways: How he related to his children—Rance, Pamela, Robin, and Jill—and how they related to him. Pure, reciprocal, unconditional love.

It was evident in the concern he showed for those who worked in his plants he founded—particularly those whom he called his "special ladies." He was never too busy to talk to them, or walk among them; or to listen to and express his sorrow or praise to them when they brought news of a death in the family, a baby born, a wedding, a son or daughter graduating from school.

He was as equally comfortable working on a machine that needed repairing as he was slipping into a shirt and tie in his office and driving off to sit with some high-level client executive. One of his favorite subjects was the pride his fellow workers had in their skills and in their dedication to delivering a quality product. When a customer's company flag was raised over a Mexican Industries plant, signifying that quality products were produced there, it was a cause for rejoicing . . .

I look upon this occasion of Hank's departure as a joyous one, too, for Hank has aroused love in all of us here today, and the only way we can keep that love is by giving it away.

Therefore, let us give that love to one another, as Hank gave that love to each of us in whatever way he may have touched us. In closing, I would like to read from the first letter of Paul to the Corinthians . . .

"Love is always patient and kind. Love is never jealous. Love is never boastful or conceited. It is never selfish. Love does not take offense. It is not resentful. Love takes no pleasure in another person's pain, but delights in the truth. Love is always ready to excuse, to trust, to hope, and to endure whatever comes. Love has no end."

As I said at the beginning, Hank and love are inseparable. They are one and the same. They are indivisible. His legacy is his love for each of us, and that legacy will live for a long, long time. *¡El espiritu vive!*

Following the services at Holy Redeemer, we left for Detroit's metropolitan airport. Although Hank had done so much for its people, that city would not be his resting place. As the apostle Paul had written in his letter to the Hebrews, "Here have we no continuing city, but we seek one to come." Bill Flynn had procured the services of two chartered jets and made arrangements for a hundred mourners or more to go to San Gabriel, California. There they would attend a second funeral mass at the Mission church, which the Aguirre family had attended in Hank's youth.

The DC-8 flight number was 37—Hank's number when he played for the Tigers. The flight number for the second jet, a 727, was 34—Hank's number when he played for the Chicago Cubs. The mood on board was more reflective than somber: Hank had taken us all on many adventures, and here he was again, taking us yet another one.

It was September 8, 1994. There was a Rosary service that evening at the San Gabriel Mission church. Hank lay in state, surrounded by his friends and family. Hank's services at the old mission were of a different character than those at Holy Redeemer. At the rear was a mariachi group clad in black and silver. Raised in joyous, spiritual song, their voices soared. The sun formed a halo behind them at the entrance.

"In the Name of the Father, and of the Son and of the Holy Ghost, the Mass is ended. Go in peace," intoned the celebrant, Father Arnold Gonzalez. A broad smile brightened his face. The mariachis blended with the recessional as the pallbearers carried Hank's casket out of the mission. He was borne to his burial place in the bright sunshine of the adjacent mission cemetery, where Hank's forefathers rest and where headstones date back to the eighteenth century. He was buried holding the baseball in his left hand.

Chapter Fourteen
The Mission

Although he had been away from professional baseball for years, Hank received admiring letters for the rest of his life. This one from a fan, attempting to cheer Hank in his illness, arrived two days after he died:

August 25, 1994

Hi Hank,

I have spoken about you so often with Linda [Hank's youngest sister] that I feel as if I know you myself. I have probably been something of a pest to her asking about you and the things that she remembered about your baseball career. She has always been very kind about it, showing me articles about your business and the various honors that you have received. Linda was even nice enough to get your signature on a couple of baseball cards for me. I thank you for them as well.

I am a very avid Dodger fan. I was four when they moved here from Brooklyn, and have gone to games since. In fact, between 1958 and 1993 there were 428 Dodgers. I have a signature of all of them except for nine. Prior to your generosity, there were ten . . .

I grew up in Corona, which, as you remember, was still a small citrus town. My thoughts were filled with recurring dreams of becoming a ballplayer. Unfortunately for me, my baseball skills wouldn't get me beyond the city limits. Hence, my only recourse was to become a fan.

Living in a house in the middle of an orange grove, with no other kids around, my summer days revolved around baseball radio broadcasts and box scores. As Vin Scully and Jerry Doggett would give play-by-play of the Dodger games, I would use baseball cards of the guys actually playing and recreated the game right on my living room carpet. Though learning to keep a scorecard and more televised games changed the way I followed a game, the names and faces of those who played are permanently etched on my mind and are among my favorite memories.

A career in baseball when you played was really remarkable. There were so many layers of minor leagues, with comparatively few slots open in the big leagues. To have been so very talented that you were able to succeed at the pinnacle of the game over an extended period of time is a tremendous feat.

Your experience also illustrates the difficulty in making it to the major leagues. The year of your debut with the Indians, you were one of only three rookie pitchers given a chance to play on the team. All three of you went on to distinguished careers and had to have been very impressive to break into the majors on the reigning American League championship team. The two rookie pitchers with you were Herb Score and Buddy Daley.

I took another look at some of your outstanding statistics. I'm sure you know all this, but I'd like to review:

- You were second in saves on the team in 1958, your first year with Detroit.
- In 1960, you led the Tigers in saves with ten, which was also the fourth highest total in the American League.
- You completed thirty percent of the games that you started in your career.

Contrary to baseball bias, your abilities improved with age, your best years coming after you were thirty. You gained the sixth highest total of wins in the AL at 30, the eighth highest total at 31, and the seventh highest total at 33.

Your .069 ERA the year you were in Los Angeles was incredible. You joined other prominent pitching starts who briefly passed through a Dodger uniform, including Jim Bunning, Juan Marichal, and Hoyt Wilhelm.

A resume that included those highlights would today be more valuable than winning the lottery every year. I hope that you feel a great deal of satisfaction in looking back on your time as a professional athlete. You can be very proud. You brought much pleasure and enjoyment to the fans of baseball. Your post-baseball career has been even more impressive. Particularly noteworthy was your earning the prestigious Roberto Clemente Award. You have made contributions to society that far outweigh your athletic career.

Linda has told me that you have recently experienced some health problems . . . I hope and pray that good health will be yours, along with happiness in all that you do, always.

I have just one more bit of doting. You belong to a very exclusive group. In the 120-plus years since baseball was invented, millions have played the game. Additional millions have dreamed of being professional ballplayers. In all the seasons, with all that effort and desire, fewer than 14,000 men have gained major league status. A very elite club, indeed.

Good luck and may God bless you and your family . . .

Your fan & friend,
Don Williamson

Some fans shared their grief at Hank's loss with the public. In a letter to *The Detroit News,* published in the week following his death, a woman named Karen Elizabeth Bush condemned the baseball strike of 1994, and at the same time paid tribute to a hero:

Unless there is a dramatic movement in labor negotiations this weekend, it is more and more likely that 1994 will go down in the annals of baseball as the year when there was no World Series. As sad as this is, it is even sadder that it almost doesn't matter . . .

Major league baseball is on strike today, but baseball itself was struck away from the patrons of the game years ago by corporate owners, who chose to package and market the game for corporate consumers. No place is this more evident than here in Detroit. Earlier this year, an out-of-town baseball scout gazed about Tiger Stadium and remarked to me that baseball will be gone altogether before it gets back to where it should be. I sympathize, but I disagree. It does not need to be this way. Corporations and the corporate outlook do not need to be synonymous with excess and greed.

This week, Detroit has said farewell to Henry John (Hank) Aguirre, one of the most lovable of our Tigers in an era when the city took the struggling team to heart as a matter of course. Hank was a popular favorite on and off the field for his warmth and infectious good humor and occasionally stellar ERA, which could drop almost as low as his batting average . . .

Henry left baseball behind and went on to be one of those corporate persons, but he kept his sense of responsibility to the city. After some struggle, he became wealthy and successful—but that wealth was the product of old-fashioned hard work. He pressured few, and exploited no one. He gave back to his community, his people, without restraint, without fanfare or marketing hyperbole, without expecting any particular recognition for his accomplishments.

Hank Aguirre once dreamed of buying the Detroit Tigers. The substance behind that dream may or may not have been equal to the occasion, but at this writing one wonders what the Tiger franchise would have been like under Mexican Industries ownership. One wonders how other owners would have dealt with a man whose focus was on the game and the people who loved it. It is even more of a poser to imagine how striking players and rapacious agents would have held their own face-to-face with a tall, lanky Mexican who turned a simple love for his fellow man into a blueprint for success.

Shortly after Hank died, *Hispanic Business* magazine ranked Mexican Industries as number 16 among the top 500 Hispanic-owned companies in the United States. Pam Aguirre, Hank's oldest daughter and successor to Hank as board chairman and CEO, was featured in the June 1996 edition of the magazine. As the second-generation CEO of Mexican

Industries, Pam has participated in the growth of the company from the very beginning, having worked in many areas of the business most of her adult life. In 1998, the U. S. Small Business Administration named Pam the recipient of its yearly National Entrepreneurial Success Award, and an SBA official noted, "Ms. Aguirre is an exemplary role model as both a business leader and community advocate."

Pam's sister, Robin Aguirre Krych, is executive vice-president of human resources for the company. Rance took a crack at the helm of Mexican Industries for a few months, but decided it wasn't for him and resigned as CEO to pursue other interests, though he remains on the company's board. Jill, the youngest of the Aguirre children, also serves on the board. Mexican Industries continues to give back to the community by sponsoring student scholarships, youth programs, and sports teams, and by participating in other community-building endeavors.

Of Hank's four children, Jill is perhaps the most philosophical and certainly the most direct. For instance, she sees that through the loss of her father, the four children have been compelled to grow and stand on their own. Some of Hank's kids, Jill says, were falling on their faces—and she numbered herself as one of those. At an early age, she confessed to me, alcohol and marijuana became important in her life. Only with her father's death did she fully appreciate his greatest gift: the beliefs and strength of character he tried to instill in each of them.

Jill was terribly frightened by her father's death. But, she added, "I can't die with him. I have to live for Ben [her own son]. And Dad's in him." She sought help for her problems. Through counseling, and with the firm conviction that her baby had the right to be born healthy, Jill turned her life around. In time, all of Hank's children, and grandchildren, may stand as strong and proud as The Tall Mexican. Perhaps in the greater design of things, Hank Aguirre's greatest mission was simply to help others to stand as tall as he did.

Hank's humanitarianism as a businessman prompted Father Don Worthy to start a dinner honoring Detroit Tiger alumni who have shown exceptional interest in the young people of Detroit. Today the honor is known as the Hank Aguirre Memorial Award, and funds raised by the affair are channeled into programs for abused children. Many ex-Tigers have been so honored: Hank (of course), Charlie Gehringer, Jim Northrup, Bob Miller, Jim Price, Mickey Lolich, Willie Horton, Dave Bergman, Reno Bertoia, and Bill Freehan. Through the efforts of Father Worthy and the Hank Aguirre Memorial Award, the children of Detroit find a champion in the fight against child abuse. And Hank's widow, Tina, started a cancer-awareness and screening program in Detroit in his honor, so that others might not suffer as her late husband did.

Mexican Industries has flourished since Hank's death, primarily because Hank left a strong succession team in place. On August 31, 1994, just six days before his death, Hank had convened a business meeting in his home. Hank resigned as president, named Jim Merkhofer as his successor, and named his four children as newly appointed members of a six-member board of directors. With equal amounts of stock, Pam, Robin, Rance, and Jill are the major stockholders in Mexican Industries. John (The Bear) Noonan, the company's attorney, holds a small amount of stock and is the only non-family stockholder. Mexican Industries remains a minority-owned business. Under the present management, with Pam as CEO and Jim Merkhofer as president, the strength of the company grows. The well-being of its employees and their families are an index of that strength.

On September 8, 1996, members of the Aguirre family—including Hank's daughters, his brothers and their wives, his sisters and their husbands, his nephews and nieces, and his uncles, aunts, and cousins—attended a Mass at San Gabriel Mission commemorating the 225th anniversary of the founding of the mission. Coincidentally, they also observed the second anniversary of Hank's death.

Asked to make a few remarks at a banquet on the evening before the Mass, Pam recalled: "Even though pro ball took my father away from here at a young age, he never forgot his roots, and he especially never forgot the Mission. It's the place that still holds our large family together—if not in body, then in spirit."

Chronology

1931 Henry John Aguirre born, January 31, Azusa, California

1949 Graduation from Mark Kepple High School, Alhambra, California

1951 Graduation from East Los Angeles Junior College, June
Signs with Cleveland Indians, July

1954 Marries Barbara Harter, November 27

1957 Rance David Aguirre, first of four children, born, May 16

1958 Traded to Detroit Tigers

1962 Lowest ERA in American League; named to AL All-Star Team

1968 Traded to Los Angeles Dodgers

1969 Traded to Chicago Cubs

1975 Manager of Tucson Toros, AAA-farm club for Oakland Athletics

1979 Mexican Industries incorporated, January 18, Detroit, Michigan

1987 Named Businessman of Year by U. S. Hispanic Chamber of Commerce

1991 First out-of-state Mexican Industries plant opens, Tempe, Arizona

1992 Marries Tina Bessega, October 24

1994 Aguirre Plaza (Mexican Industries headquarters) dedicated, August 3
Dies September 5, Bloomfield Hills, Michigan

Hank Aguirre's Baseball Stats

Henry John (Hank) Aguirre.

Minor league/farm teams (1951–1957): Duluth, Bakersfield, Peoria, Reading, Indianapolis, San Diego.

Major League Debut: September 10, 1955.

Major League (1955–1970):

- Cleveland Indians (AL), 1955–1957
- Detroit Tigers (AL), 1958–1967
- Los Angeles Dodgers (NL), 1968
- Chicago Cubs (NL), 1969–1970.

Height: 6 feet, 4 inches.

Weight: 220 lbs.

Bats: Right.

Throws: Left.

Lowest ERA in AL, 1962; named to All-Star Team.

Pitching and "Information and Services" Coach, Chicago Cubs, 1971–1974.

Manager, Tucson Toros (AAA farm club for Oakland Athletics), 1975–1976.

Hank's Career Pitching Highlights

Year	Team	League	Wins	Losses	Shutouts	Saves	ERA
1955	Indians	American	2	0	1	0	1.42
1956	Indians	American	3	5	1	1	3.72
1957	Indians	American	1	1	0	0	5.75
1958	Tigers	American	3	4	0	5	3.75
1959	Tigers	American	0	0	0	0	3.38
1960	Tigers	American	5	3	0	10	2.85
1961	Tigers	American	4	4	0	8	3.25
1962	Tigers	American	16	8	2	3	2.21
1963	Tigers	American	14	15	3	0	3.67
1964	Tigers	American	5	10	0	1	3.79
1965	Tigers	American	14	10	2	0	3.59
1966	Tigers	American	3	9	0	0	3.82
1967	Tigers	American	0	1	0	0	2.40
1968	Dodgers	National	1	2	0	3	0.69
1969	Cubs	National	1	0	0	1	2.60
1970	Cubs	National	3	0	0	1	4.50
TOTAL			75	72	9	33	3.24

Glossary

All-Star Game   Annual game between those American and National League players who have been selected as the best in their position in their respective leagues. (Hank pitched three innings in the 1962 All-Star game.)

American League   Founded in 1901, one of the two major leagues of U. S. professional baseball teams. The other is the National League, founded in 1876. (Hank spent most of his career in the American League's Cleveland Indians and Detroit Tigers, and closed out his playing career in the National League's Los Angeles Dodgers and Chicago Cubs.)

Batting Average (BA)   The total number of hits a player gets, divided by his at-bats (that is, the number of times he comes to the plate).

Curveball   A ball pitched with a curving spin and trajectory. When thrown by a left-handed pitcher (such as Hank), a regular curveball breaks away from a left-handed hitter. See *screwball.*

Earned Run Average (ERA)   The average number of earned runs allowed by a pitcher every nine innings. (An *earned run* is one scored before the third putout of the inning, and one for which the pitcher is held responsible.) The lower the ERA, the better, and any ERA below 4.00 is considered excellent. Hank's in 1962 was 2.21, and his career ERA was 3.24.

Fast ball   A pitch thrown at full speed—for some professionals, this can be around 100 miles per hour.

Relief Pitcher   A pitcher who replaces another during a game. (The pitcher who begins the game is called the *starting pitcher;* and the starting pitcher must pitch at least five complete innings to be credited with a win.) There may be more than one relief pitcher in a game, and few games today are played without one.

Save   Credit given to the relief pitcher for entering a game with his team ahead and preserving that lead for a victory. If the starting pitcher did not pitch five complete innings, however, the relief pitcher is credited with a full *win* rather than a save.

Screwball   A reverse curveball, achieved by snapping the wrist in the opposite direction of the standard curveball snap. Hank was known for his screwball pitches. The screwball tends to be very tough on a pitcher's arm.

Shutout   A win in which the opposing team is kept from scoring at all.

Slider   A pitch that combines elements of the *fast ball* and *curve,* breaking just before it reaches the batter. Like screwballs, throwing sliders can be tough on a pitcher's arm.

Index

A

Aaron, Hank, 92
Ackerman, Al, 25
Aguirre, Barbara Harter, 17-22, 27-28, 32, 48, 64, 90, 109, 113, 132
Aguirre, Fred, 7, 8, 9, 10, 27, 30, 82
Aguirre, Helen, 7, 8, 10, 19, 82
Aguirre, Jill, 28, 32, 90, 105, 143, 144
Aguirre, Joseph, 5, 6-7, 7-8, 9-10, 11, 12, 15, 82
Aguirre, Leno San Roman, 5, 6
Aguirre, Linda, 7, 82, 139, 141
Aguirre, Pamela (Pam), 28, 65, 67, 90, 105, 107, 129, 142-143, 144, 145
Aguirre, Rance, 28, 32, 33, 64-65, 89, 90, 105, 108, 129, 143, 144
Aguirre, Richard, 7, 27, 82, 131-132
Aguirre, Robin. *See* Krych, Robin Aguirre
Aguirre, Tina Bessega, 113, 115, 120, 121, 128, 130, 131, 132, 135, 144
Aguirre Plaza, 97-98, 102, 106
All-Star Team (American League), 1, 14, 30, 45-46, 133
Alva [Aguirre], Jenny, 7, 82
Ambassador Bridge, 57, 63-64, 77, 97, 108
Archer, [Mayor] Dennis, 126, 127
Azusa (California), 3, 6, 8

B

Banks, Ernie, 28, 51, 92
Batista, Fulgencio, 21
Batting Average (BA), 25, 26-27, 31, 86
Berra, Yogi, 46
Bertoia, Reno, 34-35, 144
Bessega, Tina. *See* Aguirre, Tina Bessega
Bocci, Jay, 56, 64, 67, 68, 69, 70, 78, 124
braceros, 6, 57
Briley, Charlie and Gwen, 51
Brockmiller, Diane, 73
Bunning, Jim, 36, 140
"Buy American" (speech), 75, 117-118

C

Campbell, Jim, 38, 50
Castro, Fidel, 21
Chicago Cubs. *See* Cubs
Chrysler Corporation, 71, 101
Clemente, Roberto, 1, 112, 141

M

MacLean, Neal, 135
Martí, Jose, 115
Masterson, Jack, 55, 56-57
Mays, Willie, 22, 22-23, 91
Merkhofer, James (Jim), 110, 112, 123, 127-128, 129, 144
Mexican Industries, 32, 55, 57-61, 63-71, 73-74, 76-78, 95, 97-98, 100-102, 105-106, 107, 108, 110, 112, 119, 122-123, 126, 127, 136, 142-143, 144
"Mexicantown" (Detroit), 25, 32, 57-58, 144
Miller, Marvin, 49
minority-supplier business movement, 55, 56, 59, 77, 144
Monaghan, Tom, 110-111, 112
Monley, Jerry, 32-33
Munoz, Carmen, 135

N, O

National Minority Supplier Development Council (NMSDC), 109, 117, 121
Neeley, Anthony, 78
Noonan, John "The Bear," 58-60, 61-64, 70, 144
Noonan, Mary, 59-60
Northrup, Jim, 39-41, 56, 60, 144
Oakland (California), 53, 59

P

Parzuchowski, Jeanne, 123-124, 127
Paul, the Apostle, 113, 136, 137
pitchers, Hispanic, 30
PSA (Prostate-Specific Antigen) Test, 35, 119

Q, R

Ramos, George, 133
La Raza, National Council of, 1
Reading (Pennsylvania), 17, 18, 46, 47, 133
Redman, Dr. Bruce, 124-125, 128, 131
Reichler, Joe, 31
relief pitching, 25, 29, 31, 43, 46
reserve clause, 50
Romney, [Governor] George, 68

S

salaries, ballplayer, 50, 58
San Gabriel (California), 7, 8, 83, 133, 137
San Gabriel Mission, 7, 137-138, 145
Sanchez, Dolores, 57
Santo, Ron, 28, 45
Schmidt, Joe, 76, 100

Score, Herb, 22, 140
Scottsdale (Arizona), 51, 109
screwball, 30
Seagraves, Tim, 125
Selig, Bud, 54
Silva, Martha, 105-106
Skaff, Frank, 41, 42
Slovinski, Bob, 56
Small Business Administration (SBA), U. S., 64, 108, 143
Sutton, Don, 43
Swift, Bob, 40, 41

T, U, V
Textile Trim, 73
"That's Life" (song), 31
Tigers, Detroit (baseball team), 25-42, 51, 110-112, 132, 133, 137, 140, 142
Tomateros, Culiacan (baseball team), 20
Toros, Tucson (baseball team), 53, 59, 94
tortilla business, 3, 8-9, 10, 12, 83
unions (labor), 79, 104-105
Villa, Francisco "Pancho," 6, 75
Volkswagen of America (VOA), 55, 60, 63, 64, 65, 67, 77, 98

W
Ward, Gail, 73
Williams, Ted "The Splendid Splinter," 23-24, 51, 121
Williamson, Don, 141
Wilson, Earl, 59, 76
Windsor (Canada), 34, 73
Woody, Paul, 134
World Series, 39, 40, 45, 133, 141
Worthy, [Father] Don, 79-80, 144
Wrigley, Phil, 44
Wrigley Field, 22

X, Y, Z
Young, [Mayor] Coleman, 107, 111-112
Zacatecas (Mexico), 5, 6
Zuniga, Gracie, 102-105, 125-126

159